101 Reasons

To Love Your Real Estate

Agent

Find Your Agent for Life

By

David Kline Lovett

Broker, GRI

#00831621

101 Reasons

To Love Your Real Estate Agent

Find Your Agent for Life

Copyright © 2019, David Kline Lovett

www.dklhomes.com
www.davidklinelovett.com
godimhappy@me.com

ISBN 978-0-9971362-1-0

Dedicated For All The Real Estate Agents

Who Work So Hard

Also by David Kline Lovett

Books

Comedy Made Easy
Your Dream Catcher
The Right Real Estate Agent Can Make You Rich
also available as ebooks

Coming December 2019
365 Tips, Tricks, & Techniques for Public Speaking

Native American Flute
CDs and MP3s

Meditation Music
Dream Catcher
Enchantments

Life Transformative
CDs and MP3s

Be an Outstanding Student
Close More Escrows
Close the Sale
Confident Speaker
Get a Girlfriend
Jump Start Your Network Marketing Business
Landing Your Dream Job
Pathways to Weight Loss

Foreword

"For Decades there has existed an acute dichotomy between how Real Estate professionals perceive themselves with how many consumers according to surveys infer the value of the overall Real Estate industry.

One reason for this perceived value void is self-inflicted.

Specifically, Realtors need to do more to convey their real and higher value. Otherwise, consumers inundated with our Industries incessant deployment of self-promotion are left to conclude that we are collectively obsessed with self-preoccupations and personal promotion.

This limited and superficial first impression that we are all about ourselves first and underserves the Real and life-enhancing value we provide millions of consumers every year.

Tens of thousands of high-quality agents work diligently and tirelessly on behalf of their client each and every day across our industry. Regrettably, such hard work and professional skills are too often taken for granted or not fully respected.

This Book "101 Reasons to Love Your Real Estate Agent... Find Your Agent For Life" for the first time sets the record straight regarding the profound value that our brands, brokerages and most of all agents represent.

We can all take pride as we drive by millions of homes in the knowledge that each lifestyle represents a distinct story of our skill, dedication, and perseverance. Even more commendable is how Realtors work without any guarantee of any compensation whatsoever.

This story, one which captures our greater value is long overdue and I commend David Kine Lovett for so, comprehensively telling it."

Gino Blefari

Chief Executive Officer
HSF Affiliates LLC
Berkshire Hathaway HomeServices
Real Living Real Estate

101 Reasons to Love Your Real Estate Agent, Find Your Agent For Life demonstrates the true value of your real estate agent. Here is what real estate executives are saying...

"In '101 Reasons to Love Your Real Estate agent', David Kline Lovett has written one of the most comprehensive, educational books on real estate to date. Sharing the most crucial details without overwhelming the reader, his easy-to-understand guide shows the true value of working with a real estate agent."

Chris Pflueger
Vice President, Business Development
RE/MAX, LLC

"We love David's book, 101 Reasons to Love Your Real Estate Agent, and not just because we love the number 101. This is a comprehensive look at what it takes to build lifetime client relationships, and it will be invaluable for both the agents and their clients. Whether you are looking to get started or restarted, or to build your business to the ultimate level, David provides the road map in a clear, concise and readable way. Congratulations to David for this remarkable work." -Floyd and Mike

Floyd Wickman
Author of my 101 Greatest Dialogues
National Speakers Association Hall of Fame
Chairman of the Floyd Wickman Team

Michael Pallin
President, The Floyd Wickman Team

"This book is a strong validation of the value a Real Estate Agent can and should provide. The real estate transaction can be complex and cause unwanted anxiety for all parties involved in the process. An experienced and professional agent is imperative to maintain order and a positive outcome; minimizing stress is a component of the job. David does a fantastic job bringing clarity to an otherwise murky process of the role the agent plays completing all the tasks 'under the iceberg of the water' as he put it. This is a must-read for agents to improve and validate their value, as well as the consumer to better understand the Realtor's role."

Craig Witt
President
U.S. Division
Exit Realty Corp

"David Kline Lovett has created a fun and informative read that helps real estate buyers and sellers understand how important it is to have a genuine advocate representing them in their purchase and/or sale.. David's knowledge, humor, and practical advice shine through in this book. A must-read for consumers and agents alike."

Imran Poladi
Vice President
NextHome, Inc.

David Kline Lovett

Acknowledgments

I'm grateful, first of all, for life. For whatever or whomever made this wonderful world and gave us the ability to live in this amazing, fantastic world. I'm so blessed to be alive at this time in history in this wonderful country and have the ability and freedom to write this book, to express how we contribute, assist, and guide each other to make this a better world to live in.

I am thankful to my coach, friend, minister, guru, teacher, and comic genius, Dr. Rev. Joanne Coleman. This book would not be possible without her encouragement, love, and pit-bull-ishness. (I know that's not a word...yet). Rev. Joanne gave me the tools, the confidence, and the knowledge that I'm good enough. Thank you.

I acknowledge Rev. Kristina Collins, Rev. Karen Rice, Rev. Michael Bernard Beckwith, Jim Baker, Jessie James, Marian Camson, Karen Kimes, and David White Cloud Burkhart, who have all nurtured, taught, inspired, and encouraged me to believe in myself. You have all encouraged and motivated me to express and believe in my gifts and talents. Thank you, thank you, thank you!

Special thanks to Shelly Greenhalgh-Davis, my incredible editor, and Rekhaa Gopinath for the the amazing front and back cover designs.

Please note: many of the names and examples written are changed and enhanced to protect the privacy of the individuals and to assist in making the points for the examples.

Contents

David Kline Lovett

Introduction

"Try not to become a man of
success. Rather become a man of value."

~ Albert Einstein
Theoretical Physicist

The signs into the driveway were clearly marked entrance;
arrows led me exactly where to park. At the instant my car
came to a stop, a woman with a lab coat and a fancy
clipboard greeted me, "Good morning, Mr. Kline Lovett. My
name is Michelle. I will be at your service for you and your
car today." Then she inquired, "Mr. Kline Lovett, will you be
having the same type of oil change as you did on April 17th?

The above scenario was the beginning of what was an
amazing customer experience. At that point I already knew
that I was being taken care of by a true professional. The
remainder of the oil change experience was equally easy,
enjoyable, and professional. Michelle even served me
orange juice and a blueberry muffin. All this and I never got
out of my car. Your real estate agent for life offers you the
same kind of service that I experienced at that oil stop.

There are at least **101 reasons to love your real estate
agent**. Your agent may be the most valuable professional
you ever do business with! Just like an iceberg, most of what

your agent does is beneath the surface. You don't see nor are aware of many of the tasks, jobs, and duties they perform for you. This book was written for you to realize all of the many and varied aspects, duties, and jobs that your real estate agent provides for you! Your agent does more than find and sell your home for you and your family. A well-selected real estate agent will assist you in every aspect of your real estate life, and amazingly in many other aspects of your everyday life. You will discover that there are at least *101 reasons to love your real estate agent.*

Real Estate Agent

~ a person who sells and rents out buildings and land for clients

Source: Oxford Dictionaries

101 Reasons

To Love Your Real Estate Agent

Your Agent is your:

1. Accountability Partner
2. Ad Designer
3. Ad Distribution Expert
4. Advisor
5. Ad Writer
6. Appraiser
7. Arbitrator
8. Assistant Escrow Coordinator
9. Bill Payer
10. Bolger
11. Cheerleader
12. Closer
13. Coach
14. Concept Designer
15. Connector of individuals
16. Coordinator
17. Comedian
18. Communication Expert
19. Compassionate Listener
20. Confidant
21. Contractor
22. Counselor
23. Creative Genius
24. Data Analyst
25. Data Base Manager
26. Data Entry Technician
27. Deal Maker
28. Design Technologist
29. Detective
30. Document Signing Specialist
31. Dream Maker
32. Director
33. Driver
34. Email Communications Expert
35. Email Marketer
36. Escrow Closer
37. Escrow Supervisor
38. Financial Consultant
39. Fortune Teller
40. Friend
41. General Contractor
42. Graphic Designer
43. Guru
44. Handyman/woman
45. Home Finder
46. Information Technologist
47. Insulator Against Liability
48. Interior Designer
49. Internet Marketer
50. Inventor
51. Jack of All Trades
52. Law Consultant
53. Lighting Technician
54. Lingo Translator
55. Listing Supervisor
56. Loan Manager
57. Lobbyist
58. Organizer
59. Magician
60. Manager
61. Marketing Executive
62. Motivator
63. Messenger
64. Money Maker
65. Negotiator
66. Partner

67. Peace Maker
68. Photographer
69. Physical Mail Facilitator
70. Planner
71. Politician
72. Printer/Copy Maker
73. Presentation Expert
74. Production Designer
75. Production/Engineer/
    Mastering/Editor
76. Producer
77. Problem Solver
78. Project Manager
79. Prayer Partner
80. Psychologist
81. Radio Advertiser
82. Real Estate Consultant
83. Real Estate Resource
84. Referral Provider
85. Salesman
86. Self-Promoter
87. Spiritual Advisor
88. Social Media Expert
89. Supporter
90. Stager
91. Teacher
92. Teammate
93. Termite Advisor
94. Television Advertiser
95. Time Manager
96. Troubleshooter
97. Videographer
98. Web Designer
99. Web Master
100. Writer
101. YouTube Star

After reading this book you will realize what an agent does to contribute to you and your family's life and well-being. You will be able to locate, select, and assist your real estate agent in making the very best choices and actions to ensure success. You will be certain that with a real estate agent on your side, you will sleep better knowing that everything possible, and often more, is being done for you and your family.

I. Why You Need a Real Estate Agent

"The antidote for fifty enemies is one friend."

~Aristotle
Greek philosopher and scientist

I was walking to my first class at Citrus College in Glendora, California. I was eighteen years old and, to be honest, scared. The campus was much larger than that of Glendora High. There were so many buildings, and it was strange to see so many people, none whom I knew. I was just about to run for the safety of my car and go home when a woman stopped me and said, "My name is Mrs. Kramer, young man. What class are you looking for?" I had been on campus wandering around for twenty minutes, and she was the first person who spoke to me. Mrs. Kramer escorted me all the way across campus to my first class and showed me exactly where my next two classes were and where the cafeteria was. If it wasn't for Mrs. Kramer, I might have left that day and never come back.

You could say that I owe my college education to Mrs. Kramer. What makes this story more remarkable is that about ten months later when I was registering for school for my sophomore year, I ran into Mrs. Kramer again, only to find out that she was the president of the school. I had no idea that first day of college I had been escorted around campus for twenty-five minutes by the president of the entire school. That is what it is like to have a professional working with and for you, and why you need to have a professional real estate agent on your team.

Freedom and Peace of Mind

Imagine going on vacation with the world's greatest tour guide. They arrange all the lodging, all the meals, transportation, tours, rest stops, everything. Every detail is taken care of for you. All you have to do is enjoy your vacation knowing everything is being taken care of.

Your real estate agent can act as your world's greatest tour guide for buying and selling real estate. Your agent will literally guide you every step of the way on your real estate journey. How good is that? Just like on your vacation, with your own personal tour guide, you can enjoy the scenery without having to worry about the details. The purpose of this book is to give you, the buyer and/or seller, an idea of what a gift your agent is to you. If you simply scan the table of contents and look at the Appendix number four, and the 101 reasons to love your real estate agent in the introduction, you will begin to sense the size and scope of what your agent does for you. Knowing all they do and how well you are taken care of will truly give you freedom and peace of mind.

The American Dream

The American dream is to own your own home. Your real estate agent is the person most responsible for making your dream your reality. Your real estate agent will assist you in finding, financing, and the facilitation of everything that is necessary for you to realize your dream.

Your real estate agent will not only make sure you are living in your dream home, he or she will also save you time, minimize headaches, and help you in countless ways. Your agent can save you from buying the wrong property at the wrong price, a mistake that could cost you time and trouble and mean you are really not living the American dream.

There is something fundamental about owning your own home. Home is a base for your life and your family. There is nothing more important than family and nothing more critical for your family (other than love) than your home. Your agent is your surest asset for you to rest assured you have a life that matters, with safety, connection, companionship, and joy.

"Action is the foundational
key to all success."
~ Pablo Picasso

Buying a property that isn't your dream home may not sound like that big a deal, but it can be devastating. Even in a good market, selling your current home and buying and moving into another is costly; time-consuming; and a huge, unnecessary hassle.

The right agent can make sure you buy a home that you will enjoy for years. They will help you find a home that is best for you and your family, not only the day escrow closes, but for years to follow. The right agent can help you see the advantages, the disadvantages, and the blind spots that you may not be aware of.

Money

It may be a bit sad, but it's true; money is an important aspect of life. As Tom Cruise said in *Jerry McGuire*, "Show me the money." According to ZeroMillion.com an online entrepreneurship resource, eight out of ten millionaires made their fortunes in real estate. It is no wonder owning a home is so important to us. It is the American dream to be a homeowner. And to be honest, most of us also desire to have a lot of money, and to be a millionaire.

There is a misunderstanding and often overlooked omission most of us fall into when reciting the Bible verse Timothy 6:10, "Money is the root of all evil." Most of us have taken this verse out of context, believing that money is not a good thing. The truth is money is simply a method we use to exchange value with each other. Money is a good thing, and as stated above, real estate creates 80% of all millionaires. If one takes the entire quote in context, "The love of money is the root of all evil." It's the love of money, not money that is the root of all evil. Understanding the verse in this context, one can clearly understand that loving, holding on to, or hoarding money doesn't work in the society of biblical times, and now.

Your real estate agent can be your link for making money in real estate. It may not be a good idea to love money, but it's a great idea to love your real estate agent. If you check out my book, *The Right Real Estate Agent Can Make You Rich*, you will clearly read that is exactly true. Your agent can't instantly make you a millionaire, but she or he can certainly make you some money by owning real estate. The better verse might be, "To love your real estate agent is a virtue."

Fun Fact

~ The most powerful word in our Time Management vocabulary is "No".

Source: Dr.Donald E. Wetmore *Time Management Facts* and Figures

Time Saver

There is an expression coined by Benjamin Franklin, "Time is money." He also wrote that, "Lost time is never found again." Your real estate agent will save you time and money. What can you do with time? By performing all the 101 tasks and more that are covered in this book, your real estate agent gives you the gift of time saved.

What one does with their time is personal. For me, not having to meet an inspector, appraiser, or carpet installer, means I can spend time with family. I can use that time writing, talking with friends, and finishing a project. You might have something that needs to be done at work and don't have a job where you can take the afternoon off to work on real estate-related tasks.

An agent assists their clients to save time in areas of their life that don't include real estate. I have seen agents pick up dry cleaning, kids, or pets for their clients. Your real estate agent has your best interests in mind. If they can help you with your kids, then you may have the time for a necessary task involving your transaction. You would be amazed at what lengths an agent goes to, to serve their clients.

> **"Practice does not make perfect. Only perfect practice makes perfect."**
> **~ Vince Lombardi**

Experience and Expertise

In this day and age, we want things fast, and we want them to come to us easily. With Google, computers, smart phones, and the Internet, we can have most anything we want instantly. There is one thing we can't have so easily, and that is experience and expertise. Albert Einstein stated, "The only source of knowledge is experience." Julius Caesar declared, "Experience is the teacher of all things."

When it comes to our life, our home, and for the largest investment in our lives, experience and expertise is more than important, it's essential. There is a knowledge that is required in real estate that cannot be learned in a book, YouTube video, or in a classroom. You must go out and learn by doing. Your agent has that specific knowledge that helps you to sleep at night, knowledge that they have gained by practice, experience, and hard work.

What your agent does for you is to gift you with some amazingly precise and detailed information, guidance, and assistance. The gift of your agents' experience and expertise is clarified by Leigh Steinberg: "Very narrow areas of expertise can be very productive."

Here are a few good questions you should ask:

1. How can I best help you help me? (Yes, just like Tom Cruise said in *Jerry Maguire*.)
2. How long have you worked full-time in real estate?
3. How many transactions have you closed?
4. What have you found to be the biggest problems?
5. What have you found to be the most successful formula for success?
6. What mistake have you learned the most from making?
7. What skills have you gained and improved upon since becoming a real estate agent?
8. What were your solutions?

Have your agent learn and make mistakes with someone else prior to working with you.

Fun Fact

~ Eighty five percent of the things we fear will occur, do not occur.

Source: Huffington Post

Insulation Against Liability

In today's world people disagree. When there is disagreement there is often a lawsuit. The person who has the most knowledge and expertise is the person who is therefore the most responsible, and therefore often the person who is the target of a lawsuit. For you as the buyer or seller, your agent is the one who takes on this responsibility for you. I'm not saying you will never be the target of a lawsuit. However, you most likely will not be the number-one target. Again, your agent will give you that insulation, buffer, or cover regarding a lawsuit.

Agents are accustomed to the liability that comes with the real estate business, which is why most aren't allowed by their brokers to open a transaction without what is called Errors and Emission insurance (also called E and O insurance.) It is extremely important to ask about this because you want there to be an insurance policy covering all your transactions. Think of it as an insurance policy paid for by your agent.

This is a day and age where lawsuits are all too common. Many lawsuits are frivolous but still cost time, aggravation, and money. We must do everything we can to minimize the damage caused by them, which is why having the right agent who carries a hefty E and O insurance is imperative.

Your Personal Guru

Imagine how great it would be to have someone you can call, text, or email 24/7/365, who has all the answers for any and all of your questions. Most people don't realize what an asset an agent can be. Not only do they help you buy and sell your home, he or she can supply you with a plethora of information.

Your real estate agent, much like a guru, can also lend you psychological, emotional, and spiritual support. Even with the support of a real estate agent, there can be times when you may feel discouraged, frustrated, or even angry. Your agent, or your personal guru, will pick you up and keep you going when there may seem to be no one else on your side.

We all can use motivation at times, and many of us can use it almost every day. There is a reason so many people have a guru, priest, rabbi, minister, imam, monk, or reverend. They support us during tough times. They assist us when we are down and out. Your own personal real estate guru will help you get out of bed when you don't feel like it. He or she will assist you to make an offer when you are hesitant. They will support you when you are feeling sad.

Real Estate Resource

As mentioned above, you can call, text, or email your agent at any time to ask any question. Imagine the cost to hire a consultant who is available to you at any time of the day or night. This is whom you get with your real estate agent. Even if your agent doesn't know every answer, he or she has access to get it. They normally have a manager to turn to, and if they work for one of the major companies, they have access to company lawyers and experts to consult. As a member of the state, national, and local associations of realtors, they also have access to legal hotlines where they can ask a real estate attorney regarding any and all of your questions.

In addition to answering your questions, your agent is the perfect source for you to locate the best people to work with. If you are not aware, there is a virtual army of people involved when you buy and sell a home. Your real estate agent will act as your general contractor and assist you and even take care of all the details of finding, hiring, and managing this army.

Your agent has already established relationships with everyone necessary to make your life easy. They know who does a good job and who doesn't do as well. Your agent knows who is pleasant and easy to work with. They know who gets their work done and who does it quickly and reasonably. All of these characteristics could make the difference between you having a successful and enjoyable buying or selling experience, or it being a nightmare.

There are so many people involved in the buying or selling of a home. All it takes is one disagreeable personality to turn an enjoyable transaction into something you wish you could forget.

To give you an idea, a real estate agent is a resource to help you find the best available:

1. Appraisers
2. Carpet and floor installers
3. City Inspectors
4. Contractors
5. Credit repair specialists
6. Electricians
7. Escrow officers
8. Handymen
9. Home protection insurance agents
10. Inspection companies
11. Landscapers
12. Lawyers
13. Lenders/Banks
14. Loan processors
15. Painters
16. Plumbers
17. Property insurance agents
18. Roofers
19. Termite inspectors
20. Title representatives

Dream Maker

Dream Maker isn't really a task that you can watch your real estate agent perform and say, "Right now that task is making my dream come true." It is more of an overall effect of all of the other tasks, jobs, duties, and various things that your agent performs on your behalf that creates and makes your dreams come true.

Go back to the beginning of this book and read the table of contents. There are 197 topics and twenty-two chapters all on one basic topic. WHAT YOUR AGENT DOES FOR YOU. Consider this: Your dentist cleans your teeth, drills and fills your cavities, and a few other very important activities. Your car washer washes your car, that's it. Your dry cleaners cleans and presses your clothes, that's it. I don't know of any other occupation that comprehensively works on your behalf to make your dreams come true.

> ### Fun Fact
>
> ~ It takes approximately 30 days to establish a new physical or emotional habit.
>
> Source: HowStuffWorks.com

Conclusion

You don't really need an agent; in reality you don't need anything. And, you could certainly use an agent who is, personable, professional, and exceptional in your life. Have you ever had average, reasonable, and acceptable anything? How was it? How was it really? Life can be challenging and sometimes downright difficult.

Real estate in my opinion is a microcosm of life. It brings out oftentimes the worst in people. With the stress of money, time, deadlines, and different sides wanting different things, real estate can and often is downright painful. You may not need it, but you deserve to have someone on your side. You deserve someone who has your back, who has the knowledge, expertise, and experience to make your life as easy as possible. This is why you want and deserve to have a real estate agent working for you.

"Be brave. Take risks. Nothing can substitute experience."
~ Paulo Coelho

Recap - Why You Need a Real Estate Agent

Freedom and Peace of Mind: the ability to feel great and sleep easily.

The American Dream: to own your own home.

Money: your agent will help you acquire and maintain wealth.

Time Saver: your agent will save you valuable time.

Experience and Expertise: comes from the time your agent has put into the craft of real estate.

Insulation Against Liability: your agent acts as a shield for lawsuits.

Your Personal Guru: your psychological, emotional, and even spiritual supporter.

Real Estate Resource: someone you can go to for answers.

Dream Maker: you really can have whatever it is you desire.

II. Advantages of Having an Agent

"In union there is strength."

~ Aesop
Ancient Greek fabulist

There are countless advantages for you to have an agent. The first and maybe most important reason is to have peace of mind. Knowing that everything is taken care of is very satisfying. You can relax and enjoy your life. You can focus on other things like your family, friends, fun, and career.

You will have freedom knowing you are in good hands. You will know that someone has your back. You will be able to sleep at night. There is a real advantage to having a true expert on your side. Your agent will take care of virtually everything real estate-related and many things beyond real estate.

Good Deals

Who doesn't want to have a good deal? Everyone likes a bargain. A good deal saves you money, funds you can use to buy something else, or to save for a rainy day. It feels good to be able to buy something at less than full price. Your real estate agent can find you that bargain, and that is a good thing.

A good deal is a lot more than the price. It's a good deal when you can rely on someone else to take care of all the details. It's a good deal when you don't have to worry about any of the legalities of a transaction. It's a good deal when you have someone else make sure that the property and all its amenities are in working order. It's a good deal when you buy the perfect home for you and your family.

"Walking with a friend in the dark is better than walking alone in the light."
~ Helen Keller

It's comforting knowing someone besides you is in charge of EVERYTHING. And I do mean everything. That's why this book is called *101 Reasons to Love Your Real Estate Agent*. You can also go back to the front of the book and look at the table of contents where you will find 197 topics. It's exhausting looking at all the tasks involved. After seeing the table of contents, the list in the introduction, and also as appendix #4, you can feel even better knowing that your agent has your back and takes care of virtually everything.

All the Signatures

Buying and selling real estate requires a plethora of signatures. It reminds me of the president when he or she uses all the pens to sign, and sign, and sign a bill. Your agent makes sure all the I's are dotted and all the T's are crossed. With all the liability involved, there is more and more paperwork, forms, and disclosures. The disclosures are for you and your agent's protection. If something doesn't get signed, or is signed in the wrong place, you could be in big trouble. Your agent makes sure that you stay out of all possible and foreseeable problems by getting all necessary paperwork completed and signed correctly in the right places.

Driver

Your real estate agent at times is your driver, chauffeur, and taxi cab driver. Often when you are in the market to buy a home, your agent drives you from house to house. They act like a taxi or limo driver. What other occupations, other than a real taxi, limo, Uber, or a Lyft driver, drive their clients around?

Agents also do a lot of driving around without their clients in the car. An agent visits a property for viewing and meeting inspectors, appraisers, contractors, builders, and maintenance people. They often have to run documents from lenders to escrows, to clients, and back to escrow, or the lender. Listing the reasons your agent may be utilized as a driver for you would only be limited by my imagination.

All this driving is driving you don't have to do. Being a driver, whether it is with you in the car, or as a delivery, or to meet the various players in a transaction, is simply another of the many duties that a real estate agent performs for you.

Your agent will drive you as an escort to view property and to transport documents. They also serve you by meeting with:

1. Appraisers
2. Buyers
3. Carpet and floor installers
4. Civil engineers
5. City planners
6. Contractors
7. Escrow officers
8. Inspectors
9. Landscapers
10. Lenders
11. Other real estate agents
12. Painters
13. Sellers
14. Termite inspectors
15. Title representatives
16. You
17. And many more

Your real estate agent can save you precious time, energy, and gas by driving between properties and the various players and more in a real estate transaction.

Professionalism

~ the skill, good judgment, and polite behavior that is expected from a person who is trained to do a job well.

Source: Merriam-Webster

Negotiator

At times real estate can be more war than art. Whenever you get egos and money mixed together, sparks are bound to fly. Unless you enjoy a good fight, and have the skills to win, you might like to have your agent do that part of the job for you.

Your agent acts as your go-between and negotiates for you. He or she will be the bad cop by following your instructions and fighting for what is in your best interest. This is an advantage because they can save you thousands. It isn't easy to negotiate for yourself. Unless you are an experienced poker player, you will almost always leave money on the table, and thus it will not be in your pocket. In buying and selling real estate, we are not talking about chips; we are dealing with tens of thousands of dollars.

"You can only end a negotiation for peace if you begin with it."
~ Benjamin Netanyahu

Having someone do your fighting or negotiations can also save wear and tear on your body and mind. If you closely examine most real estate agents, you will often see someone who is very stressed out and fatigued. Constant, raging battles are a major reason why they look a little worn-out. I know after my first couple of years in real estate I grew some gray hair.

The most important reason for having a real estate agent fight your battles and negotiate for you comes down to efficiency and boldness. We can more easily stand firm on the price and terms for someone else. I didn't want to know how flexible my clients might be on price or terms. I would tell my clients, "Don't tell me what price you would be willing to accept." In not knowing my clients' flexibility I could be sincere when negotiating for them. Having your agent do the negotiating for you will help you save thousands in both buying and selling.

Here is a list of just some of the areas your agent will negotiate for you:

1. Clean-up
2. Closing dates
3. Contracts
4. Commissions
5. Considerations
6. Escrow
7. Fixtures
8. Interest rates
9. Move-in dates
10. Movers
11. Personal property
12. Price
13. Rental agreements
14. Rent back
15. Repairs
16. Termite
17. Terms

Counselor

Please don't take buying and selling your home too lightly. You are dealing with, foremost, the largest investment of your life. Moving from one home to another is also a very important aspect of one's life. Having someone who knows every aspect of real estate can be a huge benefit for you! You can call your agent an amateur psychologist, a caring friend, a counselor, or your real estate agent. When dealing with an agent, he or she can be invaluable to you as a counselor.

There are many aspects of a transaction that can go amiss. Did I buy the right property? Use the best lender? Did I get the lowest interest rate and best loan available? Did I pay a fair price? Why did he or she say or do that?

Your real estate agent can talk to you about anything that's on your mind and serve as your counselor for free! Your agent is familiar with the details of your loan, property, costs, time, considerations, the personalities involved, and much more.

Since your agent understands everything, it is only natural for you to talk to them about it. The following is a list of some of the benefits of talking candidly to your agent.

Your agent will assist you by:

1. allowing you to express your concerns.
2. assisting you in choosing the best available options.
3. assisting you in seeing your choices.
4. being there so you can simply talk about what matters to you.
5. coming up with solutions to problems.
6. giving you space to state your frustrations.
7. helping you see the bigger picture.

FUN FACT !

Fun Fact

~ Taking 5 minutes per day, 5 days per week to create one idea per day to improve one's job will create 1,250 improvements to a job over a 5 year period.

Source: Jack Canfield
The Success Principles

Stager

A stager is someone who assists you when selling your home to make your home look beautiful. The idea is to make the property look appealing to the person who is viewing it. The main considerations to concentrate on are color, clean, and clutter. By color I also mean light. You don't buy what you can't see. A property needs to have all the drapes open and lights on. And just like an outfit, one wants to have things that the colors match. The drapes, bedspreads, pillows, and even pictures need to go together.

Fun Fact

~ People rarely used soap to wash their bodies until the late 19th century. It was usually made from animal fats and ashes and was too harsh for bodies; the gentler alternative, made with olive oil, was too expensive for most people.

Source: Katherine Ashenburg
The Dirt on Clean

Clean and clutter are just what you think. For a home to be staged and ready for viewing, it must be sparkling clean. That means the floors, countertops, windows, mirrors, everything must be spotless. The property needs to pass the white-glove inspection. That is the inspection where someone passes a white glove over the top of the light fixture to see if there is any dust. By clean I mean everything, everywhere needs to sparkle.

Clutter means that a property needs to be free of stuff; personal items need to be put away, or thrown away. Every corner of the home needs to be free of clutter. It will make a world of difference and will also make the property look larger without so many items in the way. Think of the model home for a home development. They are perfectly staged for showing. You will feel better living in a home that is clean and free of clutter.

The difference between a property that is staged and not staged can be thousands of dollars. Your agent is an expert at staging a property for the highest sales price possible. Until you can see the before and after picture when a home is staged, you will not realize how much of an impact having a clean, orderly space can be.

To give you an idea, you can do the following simple exercise. If your dresser isn't already crowded on the top, put some more of your things on it. Take a picture of how it looks and note how it makes you feel. Now remove all but three items off the top of your dresser. Arrange those three items in the places that make you feel the best. Take another picture and compare how you feel about it now. You should feel more relaxed and peaceful with all the clutter removed. Imagine the difference staging an entire home.

Conclusion

Let's be honest, once you have a professional real estate agent you'll never go back. I remember when I moved last, I didn't realize how bad it was where I used to live until I moved somewhere else. I counted ten or twelve reasons that my new place of residence was superior to my old one. It is the same way with relationships and with your agent. If you never had a real estate agent to work with, how would you know what it was like to have an amazing agent assisting you? You would get used to having a mediocre real estate agent and think that was normal.

This is why this book, *101 Reasons to Love Your Real Estate Agent,* was written. So you will know the advantages of having an exceptional real estate agent on your side to make your life not only easy but a pleasure. So much of the job of an agent is below the service. With this book you can appreciate them and also better utilize their services.

Recap - Advantages of Having an Agent

Good Deals: you will have good deals and have a better chance to buy low and sell high.

All the Signatures: your agent will make sure all the paperwork is in order.

Driver: you will have your own driver.

Negotiator: an agent is an expert in negotiating the best contracts for you.

Counselor: someone to assist you when things seem out of control.

Stager: making a home most attractive for a buyer.

III. How to Select Your Agent

"It is our choices, Harry, that show what we truly are, far more than our abilities."

~ J.K. Rowling
Harry Potter and the Chamber of Secrets

There are several points you need to consider when selecting your real estate agent. You may not realize how close of a relationship and bond develops between you and your agent during the course of a real estate transaction. You will be working daily with him or her, dealing directly with your home and financial future. As you are making such a large commitment in your time and treasure, choosing the best possible agent for you, your family, and your future is imperative.

Personality

After twenty years and about 275 transactions, I can tell you that it makes a huge difference who you work with. Working with the wrong agent can make you wish you never got involved with real estate. It is the same with any relationship, if you are going to be interacting with someone on almost a daily basis for several months, it only makes sense to work with someone who is pleasant to be around.

> **"The characteristics of an authentically empowered personality are humbleness, clarity, forgiveness and love."**
> **~ Gary Zukav**

We had an agent in our office named Albert. He was intelligent and a genuinely good person who wanted to be a good real estate agent. One day his clients Ron and Jenny came into the office when Albert was not there and confided in me. It had nothing to do with real estate; it was just that Albert was very direct and didn't really listen to what Ron or Jenny would say. Albert would guess what Ron and Jenny meant. Albert didn't slow down to hear what they were trying to communicate. The result was he showed them homes in price ranges, neighborhoods, and cities that they didn't want. In short, he wasted their time.

Albert was like this in most all his conversations. Albert did most of the talking, and the line of conversations was not consistent. There was no flow to the conversations, with little understanding between the parties. In short, Albert wasn't fun to be around, talk to, or do business with. The communications were not landing. Ron and Jenny wanted an agent who could hear what they said and who seemed to care about their needs.

Make sure you have several conversations with your potential real estate agent before you make a selection. Schedule a face-to-face interview. (There is more on the interview in chapter 21 and appendices #1, 2, and 3). Notice how your potential agent listens to you. Do you feel that he or she understands you? Do they pay attention from where you are, or where they see you? Does it seem they are steering you to what they think you want? Follow your intuition; you will know if their personality will mesh with yours. Take your time, have several conversations, and remember, you don't have to make a decision right away. If you do decide too soon, you might regret it, like Ron and Jerry did.

"The starting point of all achievement is desire."
~ Napoleon Hill

Busy or Not

Do you want an agent who is busy all the time, or do you want an agent who has all the time in the world to help you? The answer is that you want someone who is busy. The expression is true, "If you want something done, ask a busy person to do it for you." A busy person is a productive person. Things seem to almost magically happen around them. You want someone who is busy enough to take care of you. You also want someone who makes it a priority to respond to your calls and needs in a timely manner.

In addition to busy, I would add organized. This might even be a better question for your potential real estate agent. I'll never forget calling my agent when buying an out of state property, and within seconds, he was telling me about the details about our last conversation. I said, "How did you do that?" He said, "I keep notes about our conversations and transpose them into my computer." This practice is not only a great example of organization, but also of communication.

When I became an agent in 1984 this kind of practice would have been invaluable to keep track of what was said and what was not said. Unfortunately there were no personal computers back then. I would guess at least every other week there would be a problem because of lack of communication that could have been avoided with this practice. If your potential agent can pull your conversations out of his or her computer, take note.

You will be able to determine if an agent is busy and organized by the way they talk to you and return your calls. If they have all day to talk to you and don't talk much about business, they may not be that busy. If they have trouble finding the property you are talking about, they may not be organized. Don't settle. You want an agent who has great communication skills and is organized.

Experienced or New

A new agent may have the time to give you personalized attention and may even be motivated and enthusiastic. A new agent simply can't give you the benefit of their mistakes, their contacts, and the acquired talents that only time can give them. There is no better teacher than experience.

An experienced agent will give you the benefits of their mistakes. One time I tried to save my client money by connecting her with a discounted home inspection, but that discounted price came with a discounted inspection. The inspector overlooked a broken sliding glass door (a mistake that cost my buyer a new door). That was the first and last time I made that mistake.

Choice

~ the opportunity or power to choose between two or more possibilities : the opportunity or power to make a decision

Source: Merriam-Webster

An agent who has the experience to have the contacts to provide you with referrals can be invaluable. They may know of a professional who charges you less, does the job quicker, and at a higher standard. This referral could save you time, money, and headaches.

Expertise is important for everything your agent does for you (see, appendix #4 and # 6 - #16.) This can be anything from including a protective clause in a contract to tricks in negotiations to handling difficult agents, lenders, contractors, escrow and title representatives, buyers, sellers, and you. Expertise can only be developed with experience. I love this quote by Tony Robins: "Success in life is the result of good judgment. Good judgment is usually the result of experience.

Experience is usually the result of bad judgment." Bad judgment most often costs time, money, or both. Why not let someone else make the bad judgments that only experience provides with someone else's time and money.

Expertise through acquired talents means that someone can perform their work without thinking and wasting time learning what they need to be doing and how it should be done. It means that someone has repeated a number of tasks enough times that they have mastered, or at least are approaching mastery of their craft. It would be the same way for an athlete who has played his or her sport so many times that they can do it without having to think about it. Your agent will assist you through your real estate transactions without having to think about it. Having put in the time and experience being an expert real estate agent will be natural for them.

Someone Like You

How often do you meet someone and you think you must have already met? This bond, or instant liking, is called rapport. You like this person for no apparent reason. Sometimes there is a bond that naturally forms between people.

Most everyone likes to spend time with people who have similar interests, passions, and ideas as you do. With rapport you don't have to be the same age, gender, race, political persuasion, or religion. When I was working full-time as an agent, transactions were easier when I could relate to my clients. During our first few conversations I would not only find out about their needs in real estate, I would discover their interests in life. I would focus on the areas we had in common and the aspects of their life that I could most relate to. I would look for their areas of interest. If they were wearing a Dodger cap, I would ask about it. Even if I wasn't a fan, I would show interest. If they had on a workout outfit, I would talk about fitness. Once I saw a license plate that said, "My dog is my copilot." So I asked if they had a dog, and we had a thirty-minute conversation about their dog. Our relatedness created rapport that translated into an enjoyable and successful personal and business relationship.

You can do the same when you are first interviewing agents. Look for an agent with whom you will be compatible. What is their likability factor? Do you seem to get along? Are there common areas of interest?

After speaking to an agent you like, relax for a few minutes and think about the two of you working together. How do you feel? What is the feeling in your gut? Does it feel good, or is it a little uneasy? If there is any hesitation, please don't -- I repeat DON'T -- work with them. Your gut is trying to tell you something. Trust It. Just go on to another agent and follow the same steps until you find your near perfect agent to work with.

> "We choose our joys and sorrows long before we experience them."
> ~ Khalil Gibran

Ask...Ask...Ask

This sounds obvious; one would think it wouldn't need to be written here, and we don't always think to ask. I'll never forget I was in the third year of a three-year program to become a prayer counselor. What I was trained to do, was pray. In my class of just four students we became very close. When I would share a challenge that I was going through, Rev. Kris would ask, "Did you pray about it?" And I would say, "No." I didn't think to pray about my own issues, even when I was in a class to be a prayer counselor. If I can forget to pray, you might forget to ask.

Ask anyone and everyone if they know any, or know of anyone who knows a real estate agent who is an awesome agent. There is the rule of six degrees of separation. Six degrees of separation is the theory that anyone on the planet can be connected to any other person on the planet through a chain of acquaintances that has no more than five intermediaries. You are not looking to connect to everyone on the planet; you are just looking for one amazing real estate agent.

> **"I honestly think it is better to be a failure at something you love than to be a success at something you hate."**
> **~ George Burns**

Google

To me the greatest tool for information ever, is Google. Just to be clear, I'm talking about the Internet, and there are other great search engines as well as Google. Google has become a synonym for searching the Internet. But I digress.

Google to find your agent and also to check out your agent. It is amazing how much you can find out about a person by doing some research about them on the Internet. Try researching yourself and discover what comes up. You will find information you may not have expected. Look for them on social media. YouTube all your prospective agents.

Some may rightfully believe that all of this investigation is an invasion of privacy. Even before the Internet you could go to the county public records office and check on a person. Anything that has been recorded is there for anyone to see. Things like convictions, lawsuits, deeds, marriages and divorces, any legal settlement, are part of the public records. Public records are just that, public and can be viewed by anyone. Anything you can find on the Internet is now public and available to view. *Please note: just because it's on the Internet doesn't mean it is necessarily true.

You might as well take advantage of Google to insure you locate the agent who is best for you. Note: A person who has been accused or even convicted of a crime could be a great real estate agent. Life has a way of shaping who we are, and those who have had a less-than-easy path can be the ones with the most to offer.

FUN FACT !

Fun Fact

~ It almost always takes twice as long to complete a task as what we originally thought it would take.

Source: Dr. Donald E. Wetmore
Time Management Facts and Figures

Date

By date, I mean date. The word 'date' in this context means go out and get to know each other. My friend Helen once told me dating was to go out and gather data. By spending time with different women I was gathering data, or information, about them. I was learning about them and if we were compatible.

Go out and date a few real estate agents. That is what this book is about. It opens your eyes to all of the tasks that your real estate agent performs for you. And, it gives you the guidelines to look for so you will recognize an amazing agent when you meet up with him or her. You can best do this by meeting with and interviewing, or dating, them. I would suggest that you go out for coffee, breakfast, or lunch, and bring a copy of this book. Put it on the table and make sure that your prospective real estate agent sees it. How they react may be all you need to determine if they are your agent.

Conclusion

There is a huge difference between working with and having an amazing agent, or just a normal everyday real estate agent. You don't deserve to work with anything other than an amazing real estate agent. That is why I spent over a year writing this book. That is why I spent over twenty-seven years as a real estate agent. This book will have you appreciate all your agent does for you, and it will help you distinguish a good agent from an amazing agent.

Recap - How to Select Your Agent

Personality: do you get along with your
                          potential agent?

Busy or Not: if you want something done,
                          ask the person who is busy.

Experienced or New: experience is the best
                          measure of expertise.

Someone Like You: we like people who are
                          similar to ourselves.

Ask...Ask...Ask: inquiring minds want and
                          need to know.

Google: find out all you can to
                          determine the best agent
                          for you.

Date: spend some time to get to
                          know your prospective
                          agent.

David Kline Lovett

IV. Should I Become an Agent?

"Professionalism is knowing how to do it, when to do it, and doing it."

~Frank Tyger
American cartoonist, columnist, and humorist

We think about saving the commission by getting a license and becoming our own agent. We think, "Real estate isn't rocket science." It seems so easy and the commissions are so high. "How hard can it be?" Looking from the outside, it surely doesn't appear that you need to know that much, and you know there are resources to find out whatever you need. We say to ourselves, "It would be fun." "I could save some money and learn more about real estate in the process." Becoming an agent seems easy. But is it? And is becoming a real estate agent in your best interest?

Time Better Invested

There is a saying, "Jack of all trades, master of none." When you try to do too many things, one just can't be proficient at it. Unfortunately, many people think real estate is an easy profession. Many retired people think they can just work part-time. A lot of others think it is easy money, and they can work at it part-time. As this book testifies, real estate is a full-time occupation. You are much better off doing what you do best and allowing your agent to take care of your real estate needs.

"Success is falling nine times and getting up ten."
~ Jon Bon Jovi

When you choose your real estate agent, you instantly have someone trained and ready to carry out a plethora of tasks that you would be responsible for doing if you were your own agent. Abraham Lincoln had it right when he said, "He who represents himself has a fool for a client." Don't be a fool.

Not being your own agent frees up time for you to do what you are best at, allowing you to be more efficient in life and in business. You could also save that time for your family, hobbies, pets, vacation, or leisure.

It's important to remember you can only do one thing at a time. Even if you did get your license, and even if you learned how to handle all the dozens of real estate forms (plus the myriad of other tasks), you still can only do one thing at a time. Why not have someone do the busy work for you? It's like the saying goes, "Time is money." The easiest way to save time is to have an expert take care of your time-consuming work.

> "My favorite things in life don't cost any money. It's really clear that the most precious resource we all have is time."
> ~ Steve Jobs

Two Heads are Better than One

"Two heads are better than one" -- this Polish proverb makes sense. You can get more done, solve more problems, and be more efficient when there is more than one person involved with a project. And what project is more important than your home? Matthew 18:20 (KJV) states - "For where two or three are gathered together in my name, there am I in the midst of them." This quote, to me, means that there is a Divine synergy and exponential factor of success when you are working with an additional person.

All successful products and services begin with a simple idea. There is a synergy that occurs when you work with someone else, which usually results in many great ideas. One person says something and that sparks an idea, and then that idea triggers a thought in the other person, which would never have come to life.

Don't underestimate the power of thought and ideas. We all need to realize how important ideas are when doing business. There are so many things a good real estate agent can do to help you solve problems. First and foremost, they provide a sounding board for ideas to originate.

Agent

~ a person who does business for another person : a person who acts on behalf of another

Source: Merriam-Webster

Here are a few other areas where an agent can help you:

1. Creative and effective methods to market your home
2. Determining asking price
3. Getting a property ready for sale
4. How to best finance your home
5. How to best negotiate with buyers and sellers
6. How to stage your home
7. Methods to cut fix-up costs
8. Methods to find buyers
9. Moving options
10. Problem solving
11. What home to buy
12. What improvements you will make on the property
13. What schools have the best ratings
14. What type of home to buy
15. Where to buy

The synergy that occurs between people is magical. Inspiration is multiplied exponentially, and real creativity unfolds seemingly by itself. You will be pleasantly surprised at how much this method of problem solving with your agent will benefit you and your transactions.

Liability

Your real estate agent is held to a much higher standard of responsibility than someone who doesn't have a license. A higher standard of responsibility can lead to being a target in a lawsuit. Is having a higher possibility of a lawsuit worth saving a commission? This liability could mean you lose your license, be fined, or worse.

Even if you do everything perfectly, disclose everything, get extra inspections, and disclose everything, you are still much better off liability-wise not to be an agent.

What are the Real Costs Savings?

So you want to go out and get a real estate license and save the commission. What are the real cost savings? Did you consider all the down time taking the mandatory classes? Note that much of the content in the classes will have little to do with you directly buying or selling your home. Did you think about the time it takes to study and prepare for the test? You don't just go out and take the exam. Count on investing at least three to six months of your time to prepare.

There are at least four college-level classes you must complete to have your real estate license. A college-level class is definitely something that takes time. You also have to take classes to maintain your license. Again, this is all time that you could spend doing something either more fun, more productive, or both.

Regardless of a person's intelligence, the test is nearly impossible to pass without considerable study. Some of it is so illogical that intellect can actually hinder your chances of passing. In other words, **don't think you can get around the work**.

Commission

~ an amount of money paid to an employee for selling something

Source: Merriam-Webster

Consider the fact you can't be in two places at once. Every minute you are working to save the commission you are not working your own job, having fun, or enjoying time with your family.

Even if you do all the work to take and pass the test, and then work to find and buy a property, or sell your current property (and get lucky enough to close escrow), do you really save the commission? Do you get all the commission, or do you have to share it with your broker? That's right, and since you are part-time, only wanting to save the commission, most brokers want an even larger percentage of your commission.

You can expect your broker to take anywhere up to 40% to 50% of the commission. If there is another agent involved they and their broker have earned half of the commission.

There is also E and O (error and omissions insurance) insurance fee of $200 - $500 for every transaction. Since you are a new and part-time agent you will need someone to handle the paperwork, (escrow coordinator). That's another $250 - $500.

You have to factor in board dues, the cost of your license, test and office charges (monthly office fees can be $50 all the way up to $1,000, or more). When you add all that up, and deduct another $1,500 to $2,500 per year for board of realtor fees, can you see that if you are only doing one transaction for yourself, the buying or selling of your home doesn't pencil out. When you add in the costs of classes, the time invested taking them, studying for the test, and all the fees involved, you are actually losing money.

Show Your Agent You are Serious

Once you choose to not be your own agent, the best thing you can do for yourself is to show your agent you are serious. When you demonstrate that you are serious, your agent will do everything possible to make you happy, satisfied, and get the best deal when you buy or sell. Most jobs are fairly simple as far as compensation goes. You do an hour's work to get an hour's pay. For a real estate agent, receiving compensation is an entirely different matter. Can you imagine working eight, ten, and twelve-hour days, five, six, and seven days a week, for weeks and months with the possibility of not being paid? Showing an agent that you are serious means proving they will be compensated for their hard work.

The incentive of a guaranteed payday is as good as it gets for a real estate agent. All you have to do is ensure your agent that you are indeed a serious buyer.

Here are a few things you can do to ease your agent's mind:

1. Be enthusiastic when speaking with your agent.
2. Have your finances all lined up: Lender, credit report, pay stubs, and letter of approval (they love that).
3. If you are selling-sign a listing agreement.
4. Return calls, emails, and text messages promptly.
5. Show them you have funds for a down payment. (Actually provide for them a copy of your bank statements).
6. Sign a buyer's agreement with them.
7. Tell them. "When I buy, I will buy from you."
8. When you find the right property, BUY IT.

> **"God comes first.**
> **Paradise is not cheap."**
> **~ Hakeem Olajuwon**

Don't Be Cheap

It seemed like every time I was cheap, every time I did something halfway, it ended up costing more than doing it right the first time. I love this Winston Churchill quote: "You can always count on Americans to do the right thing - after they've tried everything else." Most of the time I was trying to save myself or my client time, or most often, money.

The example I brought up in the previous chapter was the time when I thought I would get the cut-rate property inspection for my client, and it cost my client an expensive sliding glass door. It seemed like a good idea to save some money and get the cheaper cut-rate inspection. The cut-rate inspection didn't cover everything, and there were certain areas where the inspector didn't even look. One area was the sliding glass door. Turned out the door was not up to code standards and had to be replaced. This error cost my client $485, because we wanted to save $50 for the regular inspection that covered the entire property.

Be generous with your agent. As you can clearly see in this book, there are at least 101 reasons to love your real estate agent. What would it cost to hire all the people to perform all of the tasks that your agent does for you? When you stop to think about it, when you hire a true professional real estate agent and they have performed the duties, jobs, and tasks listed in this book, they have earned their full commission.

Salesmanship

~ the skill of persuading people to buy things or to accept or agree to something

Source: Merriam-Webster

Conclusion

What President Lincoln said in his quote, "He who represents himself has a fool for a client," was that one person can't do everything, and certainly can't do everything well. Trying to take on all the jobs, duties, and tasks of an agent and to do them well is not practical. This leads to this well-known figure of speech: "Jack of all trades, master of none." You already have your own life, job, hobbies, family, and expertise. When you spread yourself too thin, when you try and do too much, you can't be masterful at any of them. The point of this chapter is to leave the work to the expert, your real estate agent.

Recap - Should I Become an Agent

Time Better Invested: you can do the things you are more suited for and excited about and allow your agent to work for you.

Two Heads are Better than One: there is a synergy that occurs when two or more are gathered.

Liability: your agent shelters you from liability.

What are the Real Cost Savings?: do the numbers, you will see it's not worth it to be your own agent.

Show Your Agent You are Serious: when you make a commitment to your agent, your agent will make a commitment for you.

Don't be Cheap: when you try to save a nickel you often lose a dime.

V. **What to Expect from Your Agent**

"Expect more than others think possible."

~Howard Schultz
Chairman and CEO of Starbucks

Your relationship with your agent will be like few others. You will be close to him or her professionally and personally. Your agent will assist you every step of the way when locating, financing, buying, staging, marketing, and selling your home. You should be motivated to help your real estate agent make as much money as possible. In return, you should expect only excellence, accountability, and integrity from your agent. In the rest of this chapter we will go over what not only to expect but to insist upon from your real estate agent.

Deals

A deal, or a "good deal", is subjective. For the purpose of this section, to me a good deal price-wise can be something that is priced from fair to under value. A good deal can also be buying a property that fits all, or most all, of the buyer's expectations. A good deal can be one that closes at a time that is convenient to the clients needs. Most of all, a good deal is one where the parties involved are happy with the outcome.

"Is there anyone so wise as to learn by the experience of others?"
~ Voltaire

You might think it is a lot to ask. "Find me my dream home, and by the way, I want it to be a good deal." And why not ask? The great one, Wayne Gretzky the hockey superstar, said, "You miss 100% of the shots you don't take." John 16:24 NKJV (New King James Version) tells us, "Ask, and you will receive." So why not ask? You can have it all, and you deserve to have it. Ask, ask, ask.

Experience and Expertise

Your real estate agent should be experienced. Inexperience can cost you money. Inexperience can cost you time and create headaches. Inexperience can cost you your dream home. We talked about this in chapter one, and it bears repeating. You don't want to be the one paying for your agent's education. For example, writing offers and counter offers is an art. Without experience an agent could add something, or more likely omit something that would have protected you or made you more money. For example, an inexperienced agent may not think to add personal property in the contract.

There was an example where my clients, Norm and Mary, decided to buy a property that had an amazing game room. The room was specifically made to play pool. The size of the room was made to house the beautiful pool table. The pool table was clearly personal property, and it fit perfectly into the space that was definitely a room designed for that use. I simply suggested to Norm and Mary that I include it in the offer. Norm and Mary really wanted to have it included because the color even matched the design and scope of the room. To raise the possibility of them getting the pool table, I also included all the furniture in the room and the flat-screen television. The seller rejected the furniture and TV but accepted the pool table. If we had just asked for the pool table the seller may have rejected that request. By asking for the chairs and the flat-screen television the seller could feel better about losing the pool table by keeping the chairs and the television. This was something I wouldn't have had the guts to, or thought of doing early in my career.

Another, example can be in the realm of disclosure. Until an agent finds out that an older heating system could cause a serious health problem, he or she would have no reason to disclose the possibility. This omission could cost you thousands and jeopardize you and your family's health. Only an experienced agent would know to ask the question concerning a heating system or to include a request for extra personal property into a contract.

Time and Attention

This is extremely important in any relationship. Both parties must be willing to work hard and make time for each other. If your agent isn't available, it will be:

1. A waste of your time trying to track down your agent

2. Expensive (you could miss out on finding or getting your dream home, or making a sale)

3. Frustrating (it is irritating when the person you are trying to reach is unresponsive)

4. Inefficient (you either won't get things done, or worse, you will have to do things yourself)

If your agent doesn't have time for you, it is time for you to get another agent.

> **"To reach something good it is very useful to have gone astray, and thus acquire experience."**
> **~ Saint Teresa of Avila**

Exclusivity and Loyalty

This is much more complex than you might think. Remember, there may only be one dream home out there for you. It is imperative for you to convince your agent you are serious, loyal, and generous to insure your agent is the same for you.

Expectation

~a belief that something will happen or is likely to happen

~a feeling or belief about how successful, good, etc., someone or something will be

Source: Merriam-Webster

You have to earn your agent's exclusivity and loyalty just like in any relationship. It's a sad truth; a person won't likely do something unless there is something in it for them. Your agent will know if you are serious or not. YOU HAVE TO SHOW LOYALTY AND EXCLUSIVITY TO RECEIVE IT.

The best way to show loyalty and exclusivity in a relationship is to demonstrate your fidelity to the other person with a legal contract. In a romantic relationship people show their exclusivity and loyalty by getting married. The way to show your loyalty with your agent is to sign a buyer's broker's agreement, and/or a listing agreement when selling. This is a legal contract like a marriage contract. It is a promise to be loyal and exclusive with your agent. The big difference is with a buyer's broker's agreement the contract is for a specific period of time, not until death do you part. I suggest making the agreement for 180 days. You can always extend or cancel if both you and your agent agree.

Yes, you're not the only client your agent has, and your agent can still be loyal to you by giving you the amount of attention you require. Most importantly, you want your agent to show you your new dream home before they show it to their other clients. Without your complete and total loyalty and willingness to buy or sell, you can't expect to be the first client they think of.

Compassion

What does compassion have to do with you and a real estate agent? Buying, moving, and selling your home can be extremely stressful. For many buyers and sellers, their entire life savings are invested. Your agent serves as a sounding board, a psychologist, and a counselor to help you with your life and your most precious asset, your home.

Your real estate agent wants to get paid for their work and to feel confident and competent with the work they are doing. For most real estate agents, they like to be the shoulder you lean on because it makes them feel needed and important. As a real estate agent, I enjoyed the satisfaction of helping my clients through the high emotions of a transaction.

Your agent must be willing to share five or ten minutes with you when you need to express your concerns and fears, or even just your day. In many ways, your real estate agent is the most qualified person to help you. Your agent is in the transaction with you; they know all the details, personalities, and problems associated with it. If you talked to a friend, relative, or even a psychologist, they wouldn't be able to converse with the same amount of knowledge and details of the situation that your real estate agent can.

Communication

Webster's defines communication as, "the act or process of using words, sounds, signs, or behaviors to express or exchange information or to express your ideas, thoughts, feelings, etc., to someone else." For your real estate transactions and your life to go well you must have accurate communication. A misunderstanding could cost you thousands of dollars and weeks or even months of your valuable time.

> **"No matter how busy you are, you must take time to make the other person feel important."**
> **~ Mary Kay Ash**

I'll never forget when I thought my real estate broker Ken Turner told me that a property was not available for sale. This particular home was perfect for my clients Cindy and David Comet. They wanted a home that was two-story with, not one, but three bedrooms with an attached bathroom. In other words they wanted three master bedrooms, and two of them needed to be downstairs. They wanted a home for both David's and Cindy's parents to live in. The two downstairs master bedrooms, one for each set of parents, and they wanted one for themselves upstairs that offered them a bit of privacy. You can imagine this type of property is extremely rare and difficult to find.

> **"Wise men speak because they have something to say; Fools because they have to say something."**
> **~ Plato**

My broker Mr. Turner didn't say the property was no longer available. What he said was, "It's not available to be viewed today." I didn't catch that it was only unavailable to be shown that day. It wasn't available because it had a termite tent around it. It was three days before I understood the whole story, and by that time the property had been sold and David and Cindy and both sets of parents missed out on the perfect home.

Proper communication is critical and as the story illustrates, miscommunication can be very costly. Your agent will make sure that you understand what is being said to avoid the problems that can arise when there is less-than-perfect communication.

If you lived every day as this Og Mandino quote suggests, the world would be an amazingly wonderful place, "Beginning today, treat everyone you meet as if they were going to be dead by midnight. Extend to them all the care, kindness and understanding you can muster, and do it with no thought of any reward. Your life will never be the same again." Living by this quote you will daily communicate love, understanding, compassion, and more. As Steven Covey wrote in his book *7 Habits of Highly Effective People*, "Seek first to understand, then to be understood."

Put your ego to the side. Slow down your internal thoughts so you can actually listen to the person you are talking with. Your agent has the ability to listen from a place of nothingness, to be available, to really hear what was being said. He or she can be a space where you can be understood, heard, and appreciated. With this possibility you can actually have real communication.

Timeliness

Being on time says a lot about a person. If your agent isn't on time, it's time to get another agent. We will talk more about it in a moment as timeliness is an aspect of integrity, and without integrity nothing works, especially in real estate and the relationship between agent and client.

It just isn't workable to have someone not be on time. In the world of reasonableness one would think, "What is the big deal? It's just five or ten minutes." Being late is much more than time; being late sets the tone for the appointment, or meeting. When the meeting, or appointment starts out wrong there is a good chance that it will also end wrong.

Your agent must get back to you in a timely manner when you reach out to them. They must return your calls, emails, and text messages within a reasonable amount of time. They also must have the ability to communicate and get back to you even when they may not have the information or have not accomplished what they said they would.

I would expect a response within two hours or less. The important thing is that they get back to you quickly with the information or communication that you need. I had a lender that I used back in the days of the pager. When I would call Manny, 95% of the time he would get to a phone and call me within five minutes and often within two minutes. I was obviously impressed. Manny stood out because of it, and as a result I referred Manny to the majority of my buyers.

Fun Fact by Todd Smith

Being on time:

\# Builds self-confidence and success.

\# Demonstrates that you are diligent and dependable.

\# Indicates that you honor your commitments and you can be trusted.

\# Sets a good example for your children and others who look up to you.

\# Shows that you have respect for other people and that you care as much about their time as your own.

Honesty

There are different levels of honesty. Remember as a teenager when you said you weren't lying to your parents when they didn't ask where you were, or how late you were out? It didn't matter if you went somewhere you weren't supposed to be, or stayed out later than was asked of you; if they didn't ask, it wasn't lying. This is not the type of honesty you want from your real estate agent.

For example, you may be interested in buying a property that at one time had a pool in the back yard. It has since been filled-in and landscaped so well that only an expert could determine that was the case. As a buyer, you want to know this information. Without that information you could have a problem several years down the road. This would be long after your agent got paid. An average agent only cares about the paycheck. Your agent must live up to a higher standard of honesty. One of the founding fathers and third president of the United States, Thomas Jefferson, said, "Honesty is the first chapter in the book of wisdom."

Integrity

The dictionary defines integrity as, "the quality of being honest and having strong moral principles." Integrity is something you definitely want from your agent. The dictionary goes on to say, regarding integrity, "the condition of being unified, unimpaired, or sound in construction." To be sound in construction is like the construction of a building or bridge. The integrity must be sound or the building could tip over or the bridge will collapse. To me the greatest asset your agent needs to have is integrity with their word. This is to have the quality to say what you will do and do what you will say.

"Real integrity is doing the right thing, knowing that nobody's going to know whether you did it or not," summarized by Oprah Winfrey. Integrity from your agent would be to disclose items that might be a concern and items that legally wouldn't have to be disclosed. They will be willing to disclose items that could jeopardize a sale. Integrity to a great real estate agent is more important than any sale.

You want to have an agent whose word is their most important quality. Integrity means being on time, and to let you know the moment they know they may be even a few minutes late. It means doing more than what is required or expected. It means doing more than what was said to do.

FUN FACT !

Fun Fact

~ When two lovers gaze at each other's eyes, their heart rates synchronize.

Source: buzzfeed.com

Your real estate agent needs to be the type of person you can count on. They need to be on time and prepared for your appointments. If they are often late, then they are not the agent for you. A good real estate agent is true to their word. They do what they say they will do, when they say they will do it. You should expect and insist on all of this from your real estate agent.

Conclusion

What you want from your real estate agent is for them to be your agent for life. The number-one quality for your agent is integrity.

1. Doing what is expected without being said
2. To do what makes a difference
3. To do what they say they will do

When your agent has integrity, your real estate transactions will go much smoother and will close on time. Your agent will assist you in a timely and compassionate manner, gifting you with loyalty and exclusivity.

Here is a list of qualities to look for in an Agent:

1. Compassion
2. Communication skills
3. Experience
4. Expertise
5. Honesty
6. Hygiene
7. Impeccability
8. Integrity
9. Knowledge
10. Likability
11. Loyalty
12. Neatness
13. Organization
14. Poise
15. Professionalism
16. Rapport skills
17. Responsibility
18. Sense of humor
19. Style
20. Timeliness

Recap-What to Expect from Your Agent

Deals: opportunities to buy property at a fair price.

Experience and Expertise: doing something over a period of time and gaining a high level of excellence.

Time and Attention: service-service-service.

Exclusivity and Loyalty: consistently being available and supportive.

Compassion: deeply understanding another's situation and point of view.

Communication: constantly keeping one updated, with a consistent dialogue of understanding.

Timeliness: doing things when they said they would do them.

Honesty: the quality of being fair and truthful.

Integrity: the state of being complete or whole.

David Kline Lovett

VI. Commitment (Yours)

"Unless commitment is made, there are only promises and hopes, but no plans."

Peter F. Drucker
American management consultant, educator & author

Much of your work with your real estate agent is based on relationship. Good relationships make all areas of life simple and enjoyable. In real estate and life, it is a good idea to follow the law of reciprocity, or (what goes around, comes around.) In other words, we need to treat our agent the same way we want to be treated (The Golden Rule).

Why You Should Commit

There is something magical that occurs when you make a commitment. The commitment could be to a relationship, a project, class, or an idea. When you make a vow, something happens within you that propels you forward. You can also call a commitment a goal, a dream, or a passion. The point is when you put your intention into a project, a plan, or a person, something takes over and things start moving.

Your agent is your number-one ally. When you make a strong commitment to your agent, the law of reciprocity will propel them to make an equal commitment to you. This seems strange, and it works. Have faith and take that first step with your agent and with anything and anyone who you value in your life. You will be glad you did.

Commitment

~ the state or quality of being dedicated to a cause, activity, etc.

Source: Merriam-Webster

I Do Mean Just One

I can't tell you the trouble, pain, and sickness I have experienced by believing the idea that, if some is good then more must be better. The tendency may be for you to get another agent, or two. You might say to yourself, "So and so will still be my primary agent and I'll just have these two or three on the side so I don't miss finding my dream home," or "I'll have a primary agent and if they aren't available I can call one of the others."

I have a rule, or I should say the universe has one. **When I'm out of integrity, my world is out of integrity.** How many people have an affair without the marriage being affected? The person who was cheated on loses their commitment; they no longer TRUST the offensive partner. The one who cheated feels guilty and acts differently, and may be more likely to cheat again. It's the same in real estate, the agent who gave you great deals discovered you were working with someone else and all of a sudden the deals stop coming. Is it any wonder why? The Universe gives you exactly what you give. As stated in Luke 6:38 (KJV), "Give, and it shall be given unto you."

> **"You always have two choices: your commitment versus your fear."**
> **~Sammy Davis Jr.**

Higher Commitment Higher Payoff

I believe this is the most important point in this book. If you want to be successful, **make a full-on, full-out commitment to your agent.** The more loyalty you give the more you will receive; it's just the way things work.

It makes sense; put yourself in the shoes of a real estate agent. When someone is loyal and makes a commitment to you, you make a commitment to them. You feel needed and important when someone puts their faith and trust in you. You feel good with an assurance that if you make a commitment the Universe will respond in kind. Making a commitment to your agent is a recipe for success.

Why Not Make Life Easy?

It is less complicated to just have one real estate agent. You don't have to remember what you said and who you said it to. You will never have to remember which agent you talked to about a certain property, a loan, or inspector. Just this one aspect will make your life easier. There won't be any uncomfortable situations where you have to tell someone you bought a property from someone else. Most importantly, you won't be put into a position of having to, wanting to, or feeling you need to lie.

Life is meant to be easy, fun, and hassle-free. Not having to worry about what you said or who you said it to will make your life easier. If you are like me you want to be honest in your dealings with people. Integrity and honesty are extremely important to me, and having just one agent makes life easier.

Peace of Mind

Peace of mind is worth a lot. You can't fully enjoy life without it. Having the right real estate agent that gives you their trust, faith, and commitment is a formula for success and well-being. When you have a great real estate agent on your side, you know that all your real estate needs are going to be taken care of. You will have faith and trust that when you buy, you will buy the right home at the right price. You will rest knowing that there are no facts, flaws, or defects of the property that have been withheld from you. When you sell you will be assured that you will sell at a fair price for everyone and that you are protected from liability. You'll have peace of mind knowing that your agent has your back.

> **"Now faith is the substance of things hoped for, the evidence of things not seen."**
> **~ Hebrews 11:1 (KJV)**

The Law of Attraction

You want to have the best possible real estate agent working with you. The more you are committed to your agent, with the intent that he or she gets what they want and need, the more you will receive what you want and need. Galatians 6:7 (KJV) states, "Be not deceived; God is not mocked: for whatsoever a man soweth, that shall he also reap."

Be good to others, do good things, and good will come back to you. Galatians 6:9 ESV (English Standard Version) states, "And let us not grow weary of doing good, for in due season we will reap, if we do not give up." It starts with you. Set the intention to simply be and do everything you can to the best you can with the utmost integrity. If you are good to others, you will be well on your way to success. As you give others what they want, you will tend to get what you want.

Communication

~ the act or process of using words, sounds, signs, or behaviors to express or exchange information or to express your ideas, thoughts, feelings, etc.

Source: Merriam-Webster

Better Communication

You will have better communication by only having to deal with one real estate agent. By staying with one agent you will get to know and have a better understanding with each other. Your commitment will pay off with you both on the same path concerning your true needs, goals, and dreams.

By being committed to one agent, you both will have an opportunity to know each other and what each of you feels to be important. By knowing more about your agent and your agent knowing more about you, you will understand what each of you are striving to accomplish.

Conclusion

When you are working with your agent you are in relationship. In a relationship one can hope for and expect a certain amount of commitment. Your mutual commitment includes fidelity, friendship, honesty, loyalty, communication, reliability, and trust. The law of reciprocity states, as you give you receive. If you want a friend, you have to be a friend. If you want to be understood, you have to understand. This is exactly the way it works with your agent; if you want to have an amazing agent, you have to be an amazing client.

Recap - Commitment

Why You Should Commit: when you commit, your agent will be committed to serve you.

I Do Mean Just One: it doesn't work to have more than one agent, once you find your agent, commit to him or her.

Higher Commitment Higher Payoff: the more you give the more you receive.

Why Not Make Life Easy?: with one agent you don't have to worry about what you said and who to.

Peace of Mind: you have peace of mind working with just one amazing agent.

The Law of Attraction: the more you commit to someone the more committed they will be to you.

Better Communication: when you are exclusive with one agent, you will have improved communication.

VII. When Do You Opt Out?

"They say that time changes things, but you actually have to change them yourself."

~ Andy Warhol
American artist

It is true that, "Give, and it shall be given unto you." Luke 6:38 (KJV), and "A man who has friends must himself be friendly." Proverbs 18:24 (NKJV). And despite these truths there are times when the best thing that one can do is to say, "Thank you, but no thank you." There are times and people who just aren't compatible with each other. It may take time for you (see chapter 21) to find the agent who is your agent for life.

This chapter will answer the question, when is enough, enough? Where and how do you say, "Thanks, but no thanks?" And how do you determine if that agent is the right agent? There is no perfect formula for how to get in and how and when to get out. This chapter provides a few methods for you to insure you can gracefully walk away from a not-so-good agent and on to your agent for life.

Make an Agreement Upfront

I want you to find an extraordinary real estate agent who will remain your agent for life. In all likelihood you will have to work with several agents before you find the one who is right for you. This is why you need to be prepared to opt out.

If you are looking to buy a home, there is a form called a buyer's broker's agreement. This agreement is seldom used because agents are often cautious of scaring their clients off. This agreement ties the buyer with their agent. If you are selling, the form that ties the agent to the client is called the listing agreement. Unlike the buyer's broker's agreement, the listing agreement is utilized virtually every time that a seller agrees to enlist an agent to assist them to sell their property.

I recommend that you make an initial agreement for 180 days with an opt-out clause if your agent isn't honoring your agreement.

This will:

1. allow your agent to help you find the right home and not just try to sell you a home, just to get paid.
2. demonstrate that you know what you want.
3. Illuminate manipulation.
4. motivate your agent to work harder.
5. sets off the law of reciprocity to work for you. (as you make a commitment to your agent, your agent will make a commitment to you.)
6. show you are serious.

No Manipulation

With a 180 day agreement your agent won't be motivated to push you into an agreement to ensure they will be paid. What many clients (both buyers and sellers) don't know is that they can amend an agreement. Most every form has an area to add details. Before you sign your buyer broker agreement, and/or listing agreement, add an "opt-out" clause. You may opt out after a thirty-day trial period.

This is what you should insist on in your buyer broker agreement:

1.   Agent to fully communicate with buyer
2.   Agent to provide buyer with properties that fit the buyer's criteria. (e.g., area, price range, agreed-upon amenities)
3.   At the end of thirty days, buyer may opt out if agent hasn't fulfilled on the agreement.

What you should add for your listing agreements when you are selling:

1.   Agent to launch the actions described in his or her marketing plan and send a weekly report to you, the seller.
2.   Agent to fully communicate with seller.

"Our truest life is when we are in dreams awake.
~ Henry David Thoreau

3. If agent fails to execute the plan fully, seller may opt out.

The key is having the opportunity to opt out if things are not working. This is not a social event ... this is business! If you are not getting what you need, you must go on to someone else who can help you. I'm talking about you finding an agent for life. If your agent is not an amazing agent, you must move on to find an agent who is.

Fun Fact

~ Happiness and stress are contagious; surrounding yourself with happier people will make you happier too.

Source: Dr. Nicholas Christakis
Harvard Medical School

Character, Personality & Charisma

Character, personality, and charisma are very important aspects for your future agent. If your real estate agent doesn't have character, personality, and charisma, they most likely are not the agent you are looking for. Your agent will need to have tact, social skills, and tenacity to find or sell your home. These qualities will assist them to get your offers accepted and to close escrows with a minimum of problems, hassles, and effort. If your agent is lacking in character, run away and don't look back. If you see them lying, cheating, or taking advantage of people, then chances are they will exhibit those behaviors toward you.

If she or he isn't fun to be around, they are not the one. Personality is important, and in most instances one can judge a person's character by how they interact with you. If you don't feel it, if your potential agent isn't completely honest, it's time to leave. If their personality doesn't mesh with you, it's time to move on. If they don't have charm, you will know it, and yes, it's time to opt out.

When Communication Fails

There will be certain people that you simply will not communicate with. If your prospective agent is not able to listen and hear exactly what you said and repeat it, you will not be certain if they understand you. This failure in communication can cost you in money and time. They are not your agent, and you should say, "Thank you," and move on in your search.

Can you imagine explaining to your agent the features you must have in a property, and they miss one or two? Missing a couple of the features could make it nearly impossible for you to find the home you are looking for.

There is also the communication of simply getting back to you when you email, call, or text. You should expect to receive a response within a couple of hours, and most times an immediate response is what to expect. If they make it a habit to not respond to you or make you regularly wait two or three days, get another agent.

What Is Your Agent's Real Estate IQ?

There is a certain level of knowledge that is required to be your agent. Your agent must know considerably more than you about real estate. If your agent regularly has to get back to you with information, they are not your agent. As you can see in this book, an agent has a myriad of tasks to perform. If your agent isn't quick with a decision, action, or plan of action, they are not the one.

Your agent needs to know real estate including: the local area, lending, markets, marketing, laws, contracts, and more. They don't have to be Einstein or a rocket scientist; however, they do have to know real estate, people, and you. Again, if your prospective agent doesn't have a strong knowledge, they are not your agent and it's time for you to move on.

There is a Bond or There Isn't

A bond needs to be developed between you and your agent. If there is no bond, they are not your agent. A bond is where you both have a feeling where you can be free to say what is on your mind, where you can open up and say what needs to be said. A bond is where you feel a sense of connection, an affinity for each other. It's a relationship where you like each other; you just get along and enjoy spending time together. If there is no bond, you won't be successful. If there is no bond, you'll need to opt out no later than the end of the thirty days.

Conclusion

Real estate is a business. For most buyers and sellers it is the largest investment one will ever make. It is imperative for you to find and work with an amazing agent. If you are not working with an amazing agent you need to opt out and move on. This chapter deals with how to discover and handle the situation of not working with an agent who is right for you and how to move on. When handled up front with a buyer's broker's agreement, and/or listing agreement a transition can and will be easier for all parties concerned.

Recap - When Do You Opt Out?

Make an Agreement Upfront: execute a buyer/ broker and/ or a listing agreement in writing before you start working with an agent.

No Manipulation: with a 180 day agreement, your agent will not try to manipulate you into a sale.

Character, Personality & Charisma: are traits your amazing agent must have.

When Communication Fails: run.

What is Your Real Estate Agent's IQ? your agent must know considerably more than you.

There is a Bond or There isn't: there must be a level of connection between you and your agent.

VIII. What Your Agent Must Know

"Knowledge is of two kinds: we know a subject ourselves, or we know where we can find information upon it."

~ Samuel Johnson
English essayist, biographer, and cultural critic

Your real estate agent must have knowledge and skills in all the 101 reasons to love your real estate agent. It may seem a lot to ask for, and this is what an agent does for you. There are, however, some skills that are more important than others. This chapter will give you an idea of the most important areas of expertise that your agent must know.

How to Locate Your Dream Home

Your agent must be creative in finding you your dream home. There are more methods than simply looking on the computer and searching the Multiple Listing Service (MLS). You want an agent who will go the extra mile for you. One of the things I would do for my clients was to look at the 'for sale by owner' properties that suited their criteria. A 'for sale by owner', or FSBO, are homes that are not listed for sale in the MLS. Another method is to investigate the properties that are in the area where my buyers were looking, but not for sale. I would often door knock the properties in their desired area, asking the homeowners if they or a neighbor were thinking of moving.

There was a time when my clients Lester and Kathy put an offer on a property that they absolutely loved. The home included everything they were looking for. The kitchen, the bonus room, the back yard, and the location were exactly what they wanted. Their offering price was acceptable to the seller. The escrow was about to close and then unexpectedly the seller had a massive heart attack. The selling of the home was put on hold, indefinitely. Kathy and Lester wanted to move quickly to get their kids in the local schools by September. I knocked on the doors of the neighboring homes to the one they put the offer on. I called the two 'for sale by owners' in the area and was able to find Kathy and Lester the home of their dreams, and they were able to close escrow and move in just prior to the start of their kids' school year. This is an example of the kind of effort and diligence an agent will provide for you.

Your agent must know exactly what it is you are looking for and your goals. This means they must have a good understanding of your dreams. Your agent needs to know the exact area, price, type, and condition of your dream home.

Your agent will know all the precise details of what your dream home looks and feels like. How does the morning light fill up the bedroom, kitchen, and den in the morning? What is the feeling you get when sitting in the living room? Can you see the mountains from the porch? This information needs to be conveyed orally and in writing! It is best to include exactly the type of property you are looking for in the buyer-broker agreement. Many average agents end up wasting your time and theirs by looking at property that doesn't match your dreams.

Where are the Buyers?

When it is time for you to consider selling, your agent's primary responsibility is to find the perfect buyer for your home. This sounds easy; just take a few pictures, put the property on the MLS, help stage, or prepare your home for sale, and then wait. Wait? Do you want an agent who waits? Waiting is not in the job description of the *101 reasons to love your real estate agent*. Your agent's job is like that of an iceberg; most of their work is unnoticed beneath the surface. You don't see what they are doing for you. Your agent will be performing a plethora of duties to find your perfect buyer.

Here are a few of the sources that your agent utilizes to find buyers:

1. Buyer calls on the for sale sign on the property
2. Company relocation
3. Door knocking around the property asking the neighbors who they know
4. Friends and family
5. From their current and past clients
6. From the parents, teachers, and faculty of the local schools
7. Newspaper ads
8. Real estate agents
9. Radio, television, and YouTube
10. Social media
11. The local businesses, such as the closest supermarket

> ### Knowledge
>
> ~ Knowledge is a familiarity, awareness, or understanding of someone or something, such as facts, information, descriptions, or skills, which is acquired through experience or education by perceiving, discovering, or learning.
>
> Source: Merriam-Webster

Are You Serious?

If your agent doesn't believe you are serious, they won't be either. You must let your agent know that you are motivated. Your agent will know you are motivated by your attitude and actions. I had a client named Emily. Emily returned every call, text, and email, most within a few minutes, and often seconds. When I asked her to get her bank statements, pay stubs, and tax returns available for the lender, Emily emailed them to me within ten minutes. It was obvious that Emily wanted to get things done and get them done now. I was caught up in her enthusiasm and was that much more motivated to find and close escrow on her perfect home.

What client do you think had priority? Emily and her dream home were constantly on my mind. She was on the top of my to-do list. Within two weeks of our first appointment Emily's dream home was under contract and in escrow. We closed escrow just three weeks later. Emily had her dream home because she was serious.

The Paperwork

It does little good to go on a vacation without your luggage. This is the same as hiring a real estate agent who doesn't understand the paperwork. The forms or paperwork were developed by the Department of Real Estate Lawyers. They have scrutinized the contracts with the intent of covering every problem or conflict that might come up in a real estate transaction. Knowledge of the paperwork makes life much easier for you as a buyer or a seller. Your agent has participated in many real estate transactions. He or she has studied, taken classes, and knows the paperwork. They understand what is needed to best protect you from liability and to make sure you get the best deal.

"Individual commitment to a group effort - that is what makes a team work, a company work, a society work, a civilization work."
~ Vince Lombardi

Law

It's not a good thing to be involved in a lawsuit. Your agent can and will help you avoid a lawsuit by disclosing all material facts regarding a property. Your agent for life will not be afraid to disclose facts about a property for fear of jeopardizing a transaction. Your agent will make sure all parties are aware of the conditions, features, and flaws involved in a property. The ability and willingness to disclose all material facts will be the single biggest asset your agent will provide to keep you out of trouble.

Your agent in most circumstances is not a lawyer; however, they do know something about real estate law. As stated, the one thing that they know to do is to disclose, disclose, disclose. Your agent knows that transparency is a key factor in keeping you out of legal trouble.

FUN FACT !

Fun Fact

~ According to the NAR (National Association of Realtors), in 2013 88% of home purchases were financed.

Financing

Your agent doesn't have to be a lender. In actuality, I prefer that they are not lenders. It is my opinion that being a lender is like wearing too many hats. It's like being a jack of all trades and a master of none. Your agent does, however, need to have a good understanding of financing and the current programs available. They must be able to help you locate the best, most affordable financing available.

Financing is an area where your agent shines. To best service my clients I stay in constant contact with who I call my can-do lender. Her name is Jill. Jill can get just about anybody qualified. She continually has access to the latest and most flexible financing available. In this case it isn't what I know, it is who I know. It didn't seem to matter how many times a person had been turned down for a loan. Jill had a method to get the loan through.

You may ask yourself, "Is it important to have this kind of lender available for buyers?" The answer is yes, yes, and yes. What if there is a home that you really love, you have to have it, and every lender you go to says you don't qualify. You know you can afford it, but the six lenders you have gone to say you don't. You may have some extra income on the side that doesn't show on your tax returns, or you know within six months you will have an increase in salary, but you can't verify it. What is there to do? You need an agent who knows a lender who can get the job done.

I'll never forget Bill, 5' 5" 205 pounds and slightly balding. Bill was one of the rare people who loved both dogs and cats. Bill also loved to eat hamburgers and drink at least four diet cokes a day. I found his dream home that had a separate den where he could transform it into a mini soda fountain like in the old drugstores. This was a dream of his, and this home had a den with the extra sink space for the bar, 220 wiring for the refrigerator he wanted, and the long mirror behind the bar, just like the drugstore he visited as a kid.

The problem was that Bill was under qualified. He was upset with the prospect of losing the home due to his finances. Honestly, I don't know exactly what Jill did, but she utilized her latest and greatest program and got Bill qualified, and within forty days he was entertaining and serving sodas and old-fashioned ice cream shakes at his in-home soda fountain.

Psychology 101

Your agent must be well-versed in psychology. There will be times when you will get stressed out and need someone to talk to. There was a client I had named Ted. He was buying a home for himself and his mother. She was getting older, and Ted, being the eldest sibling took it upon himself to care for his mother. We found a home that was well-suited for both of them. Quiet neighborhood, close to the freeway for Ted to travel to work, and an oak tree in the back for his mom's favorite hobby, sitting under a tree and reading.

Ted had a problem with the carpet. The seller was also an older woman who had lived there for over forty years and the carpet was almost that old. The idea of buying the home and then changing the carpet, for some reason, was unacceptable to Ted. After almost canceling the deal, I helped Ted get a new carpet. Ted was happy and we closed escrow. A few weeks later, Ted's mom told me in private that the old carpet was the same design that Ted's favorite uncle fell and died on during a heart attack when Ted was nine.

You never know what it may take for you to get your dream home. With Ted, it was a new carpet. Your agent will be there for you to help you through the difficult times. There are many different and varied personalities, egos, and temperaments to contend with on the journey to your dream home. The more your agent understands how to handle diverse personalities and situations, the easier it will be for you.

Skills to Close an Escrow

Many if not most transactions or escrows don't close easily, even when people are working and striving to do their best. Many of us have a scarcity mentality. We may believe there isn't enough to go around, and we may unconsciously say to ourselves, "I need mine and you don't matter." This is a natural state for humans. We are built to survive, and unfortunately, we often don't believe there is enough to go around. This false belief in scarcity causes a lot of unnecessary problems when closing a real estate transaction.

With the human condition stated above, it is easy to see how it can be a problem and that there would be a special, unique, and multifaceted skill set required to close transactions consistently.

"The true sign of intelligence is not knowledge but imagination."
~ Albert Einstein

Here are a few of the required skills:

1. Ability to see a situation from different perspectives
2. Ability to think creatively outside the box for solutions
3. A calm disposition in the face of hostility and disagreement
4. A love of what they are doing
5. A willingness to focus on solutions rather than being right
6. Communication
7. Patience to talk with and understand all sides
8. The generosity to give more than may be considered fair
9. The skills to get things done
10. To be unstoppable

If a transaction doesn't close, everyone loses. It has all been just a huge waste of time, effort, and money. There may be no skill more valuable for your agent to have than the ability to close an escrow.

Conclusion

This chapter covered the basic skills that your agent must have. How to locate the buyers, real estate law, and the skills to close an escrow are at the top of the list. Motivation on your part will play a role in their motivation to assist you. The fundamentals of the job are the paperwork and financing. With all the stress involved in buying or selling what is for most the largest investments of their lives, having an agent who is versed in psychology is paramount. Lastly, the ability to close a transaction makes all the difference.

"Definiteness of purpose is the starting point of all achievement."
~ W. Clement Stone

Recap - What Your Agent Must Know

How to Locate Your Dream Home: your agent will go the extra mile to find the perfect property for you.

Where are the Buyers?: your agent will utilize many different methods to locate buyers.

Are You Serious?: when you are serious, your agent will be serious.

The Paperwork: having all the paperwork in order can save you time, trouble, and treasure.

Law: your agent has an understanding of the law and can assist you to avoid lawsuits.

Financing: knowing the best methods of financing is critical.

Psychology 101 there will be times you need someone to talk to.

Skills to Close an Escrow: your agent has the skills to close even the most difficult escrows.

IX. Salesmanship

"Timid salesmen have skinny kids."

~ Zig Ziglar
Motivational Speaker

This may sound obvious, but a real estate agent needs to be a great salesperson. There is an art to sales. There are so many skills that your agent must possess, salesmanship seems too obvious. When you stop and think about it, selling is the most important and often overlooked aspect of real estate. Selling is unnatural; it is not normal to put yourself at risk and ask for the sale. Being what could be a book on its own, we will just go over the basic skills regarding the salesmanship skills that your agent for life utilizes for you.

Closer

A real estate agent with the skills to close the sale is paramount. If you are buying you want to have an agent who can help you see that your dream home is indeed your dream home. When you find the perfect home you want your agent to get your offer and terms accepted by the seller. You may think the sales price is the sales price or a closing date is just a closing date. Sometimes the ability to close makes all the difference.

Amy and Bill Stevens were newly married. Both were in their early forties and married for the second time. Amy was pregnant and, having miscarried a child on her first marriage, and in her early forties she was understandably nervous. Desiring to have a successful pregnancy made it imperative to negotiate a closing date to be as soon as possible. This would allow time to give Amy time to settle in, get the home organized (including the baby's room), get rested, and relax to ensure a successful pregnancy and a healthy and happy baby.

My ability to negotiate and close on Amy and Bill's desired closing date was imperative. I'm happy to report we did negotiate the perfect closing date, despite the initial desires of the seller wanting an extended closing date to coincide with their anniversary. We were able to close in twenty-two days, eight days prior to Amy giving birth to a happy and healthy baby girl, Joanne.

Your agent's ability to close is also important when time to sell. You as a seller want to sell for the highest possible price. There are many other times you will want your agent to have closing skills. He or she will assist you with movers, termite inspectors, repairs, appraisers, and much more.

Your agent's ability to close can and will save you time and make you money. As was the case with Amy and Bill, your agent's ability to close will save you headaches, sleepless nights, and nervousness. Closing is just another aspect of your agent's job.

Listener

Your agent must be skilled in asking questions and in asking the right questions. He or she needs to listen to what is said, what is the intention of what is said, and what is the emotion behind it. Your agent then must be skilled at restating what was said, implied, and the emotion behind it. Having the skill to restate not only ensures that there is understanding, it will make the person they are talking to feel acknowledged and listened to.

I was amazed at how much other people had to say when I gave them an opportunity. By allowing you to state your real estate needs and by simply listening to you, your agent is ensuring:

1. Everyone involved feels that they have been heard.
2. There is rapport built between all the parties involved in your transaction.
3. There is a development of likability, trust, and understanding toward your agent.
4. There will be an increased understanding and communication.
5. When your agent is liked and trusted, your agent can negotiate for your best interests.
6. You know that your needs are being understood and addressed.
7. You save time and money with fewer headaches.
8. You will be able to sleep better and have more quality time for yourself and your family.
9. You will feel heard, honored, and respected.

When you have an agent who is skilled in listening, they will be asking the right questions. These questions will be based on what was just said. If, for instance, you tell your agent that your daughter has a school play on April 7th, your agent will ask if closing escrow after that date would work better for you and your family.

Your agent will also be listening for what isn't said. This may sound strange and even bizarre; however, there is a lot that is said between the lines. Your real estate agent will pick up on this and can address an issue prior to it becoming an issue.

Salesmanship

~ The skill of persuading people to buy things or to accept or agree.

Source: Merriam-Webster

Presentation

What I'm referring to is your real estate agent's physical presentation. Not just how they dress, but their overall presentation of themselves, including how they carry and express themselves.

The presentation also includes your agent's style. This may sound a bit unimportant and even trivial; however, they are representing you and your real estate business. If they are representing you, there is a responsibility to present you in the very best light.

Let me give you an example; Jerry was an agent in an office I worked at. Jerry was in his early forties but looked like he was in his mid-fifties. His hair was usually uncombed; his shirt was often untucked and wrinkled. Jerry often had a bead of sweat dripping off his brow. He was constantly out of breath, perhaps due to his heart overworking because he was 75-100 pounds overweight. Jerry was also very direct and seemed harsh when talking with people. Needless to say, Jerry didn't have a stellar presentation.

Jerry had some clients whom I'll never forget, John and Alice, a brother and sister from Arizona who came to take care of their grandmother's affairs in Los Angeles. Selling her home was the last item they needed to complete. It was emotional for them, so they wanted to have a simple, easy, and fast sale.

It was a beautiful Saturday morning and a couple came into the office asking about their grandmother's home. From the back of the office I could see the wife whispered something to her husband and a few minutes later they were out the door of the office. It just so happened that when I went out to lunch at a restaurant a few doors from the office, I was sitting in the next booth to the same couple. I overheard the woman say, "I don't trust an agent to take care of our future home, who can't take care of himself." John and Alice may have lost a buyer simply due to the poor presentation of Jerry.

Presentation Skills

There is the presentation of your agent and then their skills and ability to tender a presentation. This includes and is more specific to their ability to communicate effectively. Your agent must be able to effectively present your offers, counter offers, price, and terms.

I was sitting in a living room with my seller. The buyer's agent Brian finished his presentation of an offer for his friend Ron. In concluding his presentation he said, "Let's recapitulate the terms and details of the offer." The sellers and I were very impressed with his intelligence and expanded vocabulary. This elevated his perceived level of expertise and professionalism and had a direct effect on getting his client's offer and terms accepted. Presentation skills are just one of the many skills your agent must possess, and one of the most important.

"If we all did the things we are capable of doing, we would literally astound ourselves."
~ Thomas Edison

Organized

When you are looking for a mate, a roommate, or a real estate agent, take a look at their workspace and their car. See how clean and organized they are. If their car is a mess, if their desk has piles and piles of paper on it, they may not be a great agent. The first female speaker of the House of Representatives of the United States of America, Nancy Pelosi, said, "Organize, don't agonize." Albert Einstein shared, "Out of clutter, find simplicity." Again this can't be stated too often. Check out your agent's car and workspace. If there is mess, there is a good chance your real estate transactions will also turn into a mess.

Rapport

Sales start with building rapport. Rapport is defined by Merriam-Webster as, "relation marked by harmony, conformity, accord, or affinity." When one has earned harmony, conformity, accord, or affinity there is a much higher possibility of reaching an agreement. I love the word affinity. Merriam-Webster describes affinity as, "a feeling of closeness and understanding that someone has for another person because of their similar qualities, ideas, or interests." In simple terms, when you have built a rapport you are well on your way to generating a mutually beneficial agreement. Your agent is a natural rapport builder. He or she has rapport with you and all the various people who are involved in your real estate transactions.

> "Some men see things as they are and ask why...I dream of things that never were and ask why not?"
> ~ *Robert F. Kennedy*

Self-Esteem

Your agent will be ineffective as a salesperson and as a person if they are lacking in self-esteem. Ram Dass, an American spiritual teacher and author, stated, "You are loved just for being who you are, just for existing. You don't have to do anything to earn it." Ralph Waldo Emerson wrote, "Self trust is the first secret of success." Your agent will understand this on a visceral manner. He or she will work in a manner that is direct, straightforward, and to the point. They will not allow their internal dialogue, (that little voice in their head), or their misdirected disconnect of their true value to interfere with assisting you. With self-esteem, your agent will get things done, get them done the right way, and get them done for your best interest.

Fiduciary

~ One acting in a relationship of trust regarding financial transactions.

Source: The Real Estate Dictionary

Integrity

Merriam-Webster defines integrity in two distinct manners; both apply for your real estate agent:

1. the quality of being honest and fair
2. the state of being complete or whole

Your agent must be honest and fair and has a fiduciary duty to you. He or she must also disclose all material defects, no matter how small or how insignificant the item is. Something that seems small and trivial can turn into a very significant problem.

I had a buyer who bought a home, and the property a year prior to the sale had a problem with rodents living in the attic. The seller had them removed and it appeared that the problem had been taken care of. The agent failed to disclose the rodent problem to the new buyers. The rodents reappeared, believe it or not, on the day of the final inspection. The buyer had a phobia of rodents and insisted on not closing until she was satisfied the problem was absolutely resolved. She was so upset that it took a month and a half and three inspection companies to satisfy her. It ended up costing the seller three weeks and over $3,700.

The second definition of integrity is, "The state of being complete or whole." This means your agent will do what they said when they said they would do it. It is their word, and they honor their word. When he or she says they are going to do something, that is exactly what they will do, at the time they said they would do it. Honoring one's word with integrity goes deeper. It says to:

1. do what another would expect you to do, even if it wasn't said.
2. do what needs to be done whether it is said or not.
3. do what you said when you said you would do it.

Your agent is whole and complete in honoring their word to get what needs to be done in the time that it needs to be done. You can imagine the efficiency and effectiveness this brings to you, your real estate transactions, and your life. No wonder your real estate agent is your agent for life.

Emotional Maturity

Emotional maturity is defined by Webster's as, "how well you are able to respond to situations, control your emotions, and behave in an adult manner when dealing with others." Your agent must have emotional maturity. Let's be honest; real estate and being a great real estate agent can be very challenging. It is not easy dealing with so many different personalities, responsibilities, and tasks. Many of the people who your agent will be dealing with, (this, at times, could be you) do not at all times have emotional maturity. Take my word for it. It can be very stressful to deal with someone who is irrational, irritable, and frustrated.

A key to emotional maturity is to keep your cool, to not have, or at least not show, one's temper. When emotions are involved communication stops. A big part of selling, if not all, is communication. When someone becomes emotional, the other person will rise to their level of emotion and often go even higher. This isn't something you want from someone you depend on to handle what is most likely the largest investment of your life.

Your agent works for you. He or she isn't called your real estate agent for nothing. They are here for you to be able to have as much power and freedom as possible. Emotional maturity is essential when dealing with emotional and irrational people. Your agent will take care of dealing with these problems, so you won't have to. You may ask, "Are overly emotional and irrational people often involved in a typical real estate transaction?" The simple and direct

Fun Fact

Synonyms for Integrity:

~ character, decency, goodness, honesty, morality, probity, rectitude, righteousness, rightness, uprightness, virtue, virtuousness

Source: Merriam-Webster

answer is yes, yes, and yes...people are people, and when there is money, deadlines, and conflicting personalities and goals all coming together, people can become difficult to deal with.

Her name was Nancy, and she was my agent before I studied and took the real estate exam to become a real estate agent. I was buying my first rental. The sellers were in the middle of a divorce with three young energetic boys ages six, seven, and ten. They were fighting over custody. The wife June wanted to sell; Peter the husband wanted to keep the property. Also, there were three lawyers, one for June, one for Peter, and one for the kids. There was also Peter's mother Janet who was constantly fighting with just about everyone trying to get custody of the boys. Janet wanted to have control of the home for herself as she had contributed to the down payment of the original purchase. The only person Janet would talk to was Nancy.

I have no idea how she did it, but Nancy was able to juggle all of these personalities to create an amicable conclusion of compromise, understanding, and mutual respect for all parties. I could see that this went well beyond any description of what a real estate agent's job should be. We were able to close the escrow, and close exactly on the scheduled closing date. June and the boys moved in with Janet. Everyone was happy with the agreement. Peter and June actually became good friends. They were more like a family living apart than they were living in a house in turmoil. I was able to buy my first rental home. Nancy definitely used her emotional maturity to ensure everyone was happy and satisfied with the results.

Well-Mannered

This sounds almost ridiculous to include, but it is so necessary. It goes with emotional maturity and is important. When and if your agent loses their cool, whatever they were negotiating for you, you can forget about having it go your way. It is human nature for someone to fight whoever is fighting you. It is ingrained in our DNA; it is survival of the fittest. We fight just because someone is fighting us.

Being well-mannered goes a long way toward building rapport, and rapport produces likability. Likability is a major factor in creating agreements. A real estate transaction is a series of agreements that eventually lead to the closing of a sale. A closed sale or transaction is what you want from your agent.

Persuasiveness

Your agent must have the ability to be persuasive with everyone they deal with, including you. Every person involved in your life will be persuaded in some manner. For instance, the agents who show your home must be persuaded to show it. The painters who paint the trim must be persuaded to paint it. The sellers whom you bought your home from had to be persuaded to sell it.

The degree of effectiveness of your agent to persuade others to take an action will be directly correlated to your ability to have whatever it is you want. Your agent is an advocate or a lobbyist on behalf of your real estate life. It is amazing when you think about it; your agent is in constant contact with others, making sure that they perform and act in accord with whatever it is you are trying to accomplish.

When you are looking for a home to buy, your agent is getting people to agree to make homes available for you to view. They are getting lenders, banks, and employers to get things done and provide documentation for your loan. They are making sure that their office supplies them with the necessary paperwork to complete the transaction. You get the idea that this is a constant and everlasting endeavor to persuade people to be in accord with your needs as a buyer and seller. Your agent is a master at persuasiveness.

Self-Motivation

Self-motivation is required in every aspect of your agent's day. Unlike most other jobs, the job of your agent is self-motivated. There is no time clock, no boss who tells him or her when to come and go. Your agent generates his or her own motivation.

Your agent has to be motivated to come to work and to be an effective salesperson. It requires drive and determination to make a sale. Most every task involves having motivation, and most every task involves motivation to be persuasive and to sell. Your agent is constantly and continually motivated to assist you in attaining your goals and dreams.

FUN FACT !

Fun Fact

~ Only 11% of salesmen ask for referrals

Source: Dale Carnegie

Problem Solver

I have a good friend named Emily. Emily is a high school algebra teacher. She considers herself more of a life coach than a math teacher. She says that she is teaching her students the ability to solve problems. She is assisting her students to live their lives, not just in solving math problems, but life problems. Albert Einstein said it well, "We cannot solve our problems with the same thinking we used when we created them." Real estate isn't algebra. However, it does tend to create problems, a lot of problems. When I was a full-time agent I would say to myself, "That's why we get paid the big bucks." Don't think that your agent is overpaid. Your agent faces constant problems not just every day but more like every hour of every day; that is without taking the weekends off.

I believe a big reason we have so many problems in life is because problems are what makes us grow. If we didn't have problems with survival we would have never invented the wheel, fire, or aspirin. If we didn't have problems we couldn't find a better home, a better life, or a better mouthwash. Emily is training young people how to not only cope with life's problems but to thrive.

Your agent knows how to solve problems. I know this because a real estate agent will and can never remain in business without the ability to solve problems. I say the ability to problem solve is the reason why a real estate agent make the big bucks. The real estate business provides plenty of problems to solve. I also say, "Real estate is the reason I have gray hair." The willingness and ability to solve problems is one of the many reasons your agent is your agent for life.

It was my second sale as a real estate agent back in 1984. The buyers, Edward and Teresa Logan, loved to vacation in their RV. The property they wanted to buy had a perfect place to store the RV in the back next to the garage. There was a driveway along the side of the house to get to where they park the RV. The problem was that the home had eaves overhanging from the house extending almost four feet. This overhanging or extended roof made it impossible to get the RV, which was taller than the overhanging eve, to the back of the house.

I solved the problem by creating a team and arranging a meeting at the property in the driveway. At the meeting was myself, the seller's agent, Edward and Teresa, and a contractor who explained the procedure and costs to cut off the overhanging eve, and my architect friend who explained the new eve would be aesthetically pleasing and still go with the design of the home. The Logans believed my architect friend Jack, and the sale was made. The ability to solve problems is a critical factor for your agent.

Conclusion

Real estate is about selling. It is easy to forget with so many other duties that your real estate agent performs. Selling is much more than just asking someone to buy or sell as this chapter and this book demonstrates. There are many skills your agent must master, and many tasks your agent must perform and learn to be your agent for life.

Recap-Salesmanship

Closer: the process of someone completing a sales transaction.

Listener: the ability to hear and understand what is being said without adding anything.

Presentation: how your agent presents themselves, their style as a person, and their style of dress.

Presentation Skills: the degree of professionalism, expertise, and delivery and art of sharing the marketing process.

Organized: having things clear, simple, and in their place.

Respect: honoring another human being just the way they are and the way they are not.

Rapport: an ability to get along and have others understand and communicate effectively.

Self-Esteem: a person who is comfortable and actually loves themselves the way they are.

Integrity: keeping one's word, doing what one said they would do, what is expected of them, and what is implied to be done.

Emotional Maturity: the skill to be calm and rational when others around you are not.

Well-Mannered: the ability to be calm and respectful-no matter what.

Persuasiveness: the skill of your agent to be strong and consistent in sharing what is in the best interest of others.

Self-Motivating: your agent is consistently and continually excited to assist you with real estate and your life.

Problem Solver: a person who can take care of most any situation.

X.   You Need a Friend

"Ultimately the bond of all companionship, whether in marriage or in friendship, is conversation."

~ Oscar Wilde
Playwright, novelist, essayist, and poet

Buying or selling your home is emotional, hard work, and often isn't fun. There are many hoops that you will have to jump through. If there is any time that you need a friend it is when you are in the process of buying or selling your home. Your home is most likely the single largest investment you will ever make. Dealing with your largest investment can be very stressful. Your home is special to you. Maya Angelou wrote, "The ache for home lives in all of us, the safe place where we can go as we are and not be questioned."

The best relief from the stress of moving is to have your real estate agent be your friend. Your agent has experienced dozens and possibly hundreds of moves. Your agent can and will help you cope with the stress in a number of ways.

Your agent will assist you by listening and offering expertise. He or she will support you with positive support and will make you laugh when you are down.

Listener

There may not be a better attribute to have than the ability to listen. No matter what the relationship, we all feel better when we are heard. In real estate there are a lot of problems; difficulties are inherent in the business. The biggest problem is when an escrow or sale doesn't close as scheduled. The major cause of escrows that don't close on time are lender requirements or conditions that the lender needs satisfied prior to funding the loan. If you are a buyer or a seller, a delay on the closing can be a huge problem. Imagine having movers lined up, schools starting, new job, or a dream vacation that you can't get to.

Scott and Karla James had just gotten married. They had delayed their honeymoon until after they closed escrow on their home, which was set to close four days after their wedding day. Their plans were to take an extended vacation/ honeymoon. The plan was to close escrow and spend two weeks doing some minor repairs, installing carpeting, and painting. Then they planned to move their furniture, get settled in, and then fly to Hawaii for their honeymoon.

The problem was that five days prior to the close of escrow, the day before the wedding, the lender added a last-minute condition. The lender wanted to verify a car loan for Scott's car. There was a question regarding the remaining balance of the loan, a car loan Scott had paid off in full. The problem was that with the wedding and preparation for the move, Scott had no idea where the paperwork was. It took an additional seven days for the DMV to get the information for Scott to give to the lender. This delayed the closing, which delayed the fix-up, which delayed the move-in, which ruined the honeymoon.

This meant that Karla and Scott had to either ask for an additional week's vacation from work or go to Hawaii with a house that wasn't fixed up or moved into. In addition, they would have to pay an extra week's rent for their old apartment. Or, they would have to forget about going on their honeymoon to Hawaii. None of these options were desirable.

There was no way to solve the problem. The best thing to do was to choose the best option and make the best of it. Having an agent who knew all the details and could simply listen was invaluable to help ease their frustrations.

Friendship

~ a person who has a strong liking for and trust in another

Source: Merriam-Webster

When your kids can't start school, you miss a vacation, or have to miss work, it is a time when a kind ear can come in handy. As the title of the chapter says, *You Need a Friend*. Your agent is the perfect person to lend an ear. Your agent knows the details of your situation better than anyone. Your agent will listen and, more importantly, hear what it is you are going through.

Even if your transaction goes perfectly, there is still a lot of stress involved in moving. Having someone listen is imperative to having peace of mind and as much sanity as possible. Helen Keller, wrote, "Walking with a friend in the dark is better than walking alone in the light." Your agent will bring some light into your life when it seems the darkest.

Has Your Back

Listening is important, and you also need a friend who will do something to make your life easier. As stated in James 2:14 (KJV), "Faith without works is dead." Works, as stated in this verse, means action. There needs to be action to go along with faith. You can have all the faith in the world, but if you don't get out of bed, not much is going to happen. You know you have a friend when they will not only listen but do something to help you get through a rough time.

Mrs. Jamison was in her mid eighties, selling her home after living there for over forty-five years. She was excited to be moving into a retirement community where many of her friends lived. They had a very active social calendar, and by living there, Mrs. Jamison would be able to more fully participate. She was also happy to be relieved of the responsibilities of home ownership.

The problem was that Mrs. Jamison needed someone to be at her house to meet the movers at the same time her granddaughter had her first piano recital. She simply couldn't be in two places at once. She also wanted someone to keep an eye on the movers as she had a collection of early American dolls, some that dated back to the Revolutionary War. She estimated the value of the collection to be over $93,000. I went to her property to oversee the movers for almost five hours. I had her back.

Learn the Lingo

Every industry has its own vocabulary, phrases, and expressions that are unique to that industry. Having someone who can teach you the vocabulary or lingo of an industry can save you considerable embarrassment, problems, and money. Communication is imperative to your

Communication

~ the imparting or exchanging of information or news

~ means of connection between people or places

Source: Merriam-Webster

success. If there is something said that you don't fully understand you won't know how to respond. Without full comprehension, you could miss out on opportunities, overpay for something, or create delays.

Having someone you feel comfortable confiding in and simply asking for clarification is extremely important. Even Google may not have the latest real estate slang available. To have someone you can ask and get a quick response from without feeling judged is extremely beneficial. There are countless terms, and that is why I added a glossary at the back of this book.

> "Friendship is born at that moment when one person says to another: "What!" You Too? I thought I was the only one."
> ~ C.S. Lewis

Respect

Buying or selling real estate can be very emotional. You are moving to and/or away from your home, the place you live, the place that is the center of your life. It could be where you raised your kids, where you fell in love, and where you have lost a loved one. When you are in the heart of all this emotion, you need to be respected for however you show up.

Your agent knows real estate is an emotional endeavor. Your agent will give you space to be however you are and however you are not. When I bought my first home I was overly excited and enthusiastic. Thirty-six years later, as a result of the 2008 financial crisis when I had to short sell an out of area rental I was sad and depressed. In both extremes, my agents were respectful, supportive, and respectful of my emotions.

Forgiveness

"Forgiveness is not an occasional act, it is a constant attitude." Martin Luther King, Jr. said it well. Your agent must continually be forgiving because as it was mentioned above, buying and selling real estate is an emotional event, and emotions will elicit odd and often inappropriate behaviors. Your agent will forgive you for it. I have experienced, buyers and sellers frequently lose their temper, shout, and act inappropriately. It was my job to first forgive them and then to take actions to assist them in whatever it was they were having an issue with.

Comedian

Is there a better way to show respect, forgiveness, understanding, and compassion than to be funny? A bit of humor will go a long way toward helping someone deal with an uncomfortable situation. When we laugh, our bodies releases endorphins, the brain's "feel-good" chemicals. According to *Scientific American*, September 2011, Jennifer Welsh, wrote, "Endorphins raise our ability to ignore pain." Real estate can create a lot of pain. The ability to raise your ability to ignore pain could come in handy. A sense of humor can help you through the troubles of a delayed or canceled escrow.

Even if you are not in the midst of a problem, it is good to have some laughter and fun in life. Your agent can make your day by simply telling you a joke or making fun of themselves. It is known that laughter is good for you. You can have fun in what you do without having to do anything but laugh.

Bob and Karen were buying their first home. They found the perfect home for themselves and had already decided which bedroom would be for their first child. To put it simply, they were excited and ready to move in and start their lives together and raise a family. Seventeen days into a forty-day escrow, everything was going as planned, and out of the blue Karen lost her job and they no longer qualified. Bob and

Karen were devastated. All I could do was say I was sorry. And then I decided to tell them that after Karen got a new job, I would find them a better home that didn't have so much negative karma. A home that didn't have such a big backyard that needed so much maintenance, a home that wasn't such an ugly color of brown. The fact that my jokes weren't that funny made it even funnier. They both laughed and the healing process began. Three months later Bob and Karen closed on an escrow on a home they loved even more.

Communication

It is important for your agent to communicate with you and with all the people involved in a real estate transaction. Effective communication can make your life much easier and save you thousands of dollars. Your agent will allow you and others to say what needs to be said, so they feel heard.

The biggest and most important trait that your agent will have is the ability to understand what is being communicated. The Greek philosopher Plato stated, "Wise men speak because they have something to say, fools because they have to say something." It's not about showing off how important we think we are, it is about understanding. In Steven Covey's book *The Seven Habits of Highly Effective People*, the fifth habit is, "Seek first to understand, then to be understood." Covey teaches that we spend so much of our time learning how to read, write, and how to speak. There is almost no training or teaching on how to listen so one can deeply understand another.

The most common method of communication is the exact opposite of what Covey wrote; it is more natural to seek to be understood so others will understand us. By wanting to be understood first, we ignore the other person.

We have an inner voice that is constantly talking inside our head. This inner chatter can easily distract us from hearing what the other person is saying. We are often crafting what it is we want to say next and miss much of what the other person is saying. We might hear just enough to allow us to think of what we want to say to get our point across, completely missing the other point of view.

We evaluate and judge whether we agree or disagree with what the other person is saying. We might ask questions. However, that is often only from our own point of reference. We also might offer advice to fix what we think the other person needs. Lastly, we interpret or analyze other people's motives and behaviors based on our own experiences. None of these are necessarily bad. However, they are not exactly relating to or respecting other people's needs.

In good communication, your agent will actually listen to what the other person is saying. Your agent will start by acknowledging whoever they are communicating with. This starts things off on the right track from the beginning. Remember, this isn't just for you; it is for everyone your agent deals with on your behalf. When the other person feels acknowledged they will be more likely to see things from another point of view.

"It's the friends that you can call up at 4 a.m. that matter"
~ Marlene Dietrich

The next thing your agent will do is re-create or repeat what the other person is saying. This does three things. First, it ensures that what was heard was actually what was said. If your agent repeats exactly what the other person says then there can't be a misunderstanding. For example, if the other agent says, "My client can only pay $550,000 for the property." Your agent will repeat it back, "Your client can only pay $550,000 for the property." This way the other agent feels heard. And lastly, the re-creation or repetition of the price wasn't the typical and often automatic argument against it and almost by magic their feeling of having to hang on to their conviction to their price isn't so strong.

There is an old saying, how do you get the cow out of the barn? You push it back in. We all naturally resist. When a person is re-created it tends to take the resistance away. Effective communication comes from listening, and acknowledgement. Re-creation leaves room for understanding, communication, and the possibility for your point of view to be considered, recognized, and accepted.

Supportive

In real estate, there may not be a higher quality that your agent can have than to be supportive of, and for you. There are many problems that occur in even an average real estate transaction. Closing dates continually get extended; there is often a seemingly endless list of loan conditions and appraisals that don't come in at the agreed-upon price. There are the endless personalities that seem to be more of a problem when money is involved. The emotions that come up can be overwhelming to even someone who has been in the business for years. For you a supportive friend is invaluable.

A shoulder to lean on in troubled times may be all you need when your transaction doesn't go as planned. The support that your agent will give you will assist you through these troubled times. Support can and will demonstrate itself in many diverse ways. Your agent will be a supporting ear. He or she will lend a helping hand, and they will take a stand for you. Your agent will hear whatever you have to say.

> "There is a magnet in your heart that will attract true friends. That magnet is unselfishness, thinking of others first; when you learn to live for others, they will live for you."
> ~ Paramahansa Yogananda

Positive

"Believe in yourself! Have faith in your abilities! Without a humble but reasonable confidence in your own powers, you cannot be successful or happy." This was written by Norman Vincent Peale, the author of *The Power of Positive Thinking*. Your agent can be your link to success and happiness. Henry Ford stated, "If you think you can do a thing or think you can't do a thing, you're right." Your agent will help you think that you can get things done were you may have never dreamed possible.

It doesn't take much to put someone into a negative way of being, and it can often take a lot to get someone out of it. There is something magical that occurs when you have someone who is positive on your side. A positive real estate agent on your side can make a real difference. An upbeat agent can give you a sense that you can accomplish anything.

Whether things are going well or there are delays, it's best to remain positive. To have someone around you who is positive is an absolute must. Your agent will help keep you in an upbeat mood.

Trustworthy & Honest

There is nothing more important than to have someone you are working with who is trustworthy and honest. If you don't trust the person you are working with, who can you trust? I know from experience life is very difficult when you try to do everything yourself. When you're dealing with the largest asset you will ever own, it is a must to work with someone who is honest and trustworthy.

All realtors are sworn to a fiduciary duty. If you don't feel your real estate agent can be trusted 100% they are not your agent for life. If you don't trust your real estate agent, drop that person and find another agent.

FUN FACT !

Fun Fact

"Not having a social support network can be a higher death risk than obesity or leading a sedentary life without exercise," explains Julianne Holt-Lunstad, professor of psychology and head of a study at Brigham Young University, on the relationship between friendship and longevity.

Conclusion

Oprah Winfrey stated, "Lots of people want to ride with you in the limo, but what you want is someone who will take the bus with you when the limo breaks down." When you find your agent, you have a friend in good times and in bad. Much of the time in life and especially when working in real estate, you need a friend. Your real estate agent is the person who is familiar with your situation and circumstance better than anyone. They are the person who knows you and is in the middle of the transaction with you. Your agent knows what's going on. They know you, and they know the language of real estate.

Take full advantage of your agent. They are there for you. You need to have a friend, a friend who knows what you are going through. Your agent has the skills and expertise to do something to impact and improve your circumstances and your life.

Fun Fact

~ In a lifetime, one makes 396 friendships but only one in 12, (33) stands the test of time.

~ Out of the 33, only 6 are considered to be close friends while the 27 are social friends, i.e., workmates or drinking buddies.

Recap - You Need a Friend

Listener: someone who will simply hear what you are trying to communicate.

Has your back: someone who will go the extra mile for you.

Learn the Lingo: you can't communicate without knowing the language of a particular group or industry.

Respect: your agent honors you for what you are going though.

Forgiveness: you can count on your agent to forgive any indiscretions.

Comedian: often in a real estate transaction you need someone to make you laugh and bring you joy.

Communication: especially in real estate, understanding one another is paramount.

Supportive: your agent will provide you with whatever you need.

Positive: being upbeat, creating and maintaining a winning attitude.

Trustworthy & Honest: what you need the most is someone on your side who tells you what is what.

XI. Coach

"Make sure that team members know they are working with you, not for you."

~ John Wooden
Hall of Fame basketball coach

There is a special bond between a coach and the person they are coaching. Real estate is complicated and complex with many aspects, definitions, and a multitude of situations and scenarios that can occur. Even if you have completed a few transactions, you will never know enough. Having someone who has the experience, expertise, and the knowledge of the game of real estate is invaluable. Your agent not only will coach you in real estate, he or she will coach you in the mental and emotional aspects of dealing with the problems that come up.

Teammate

The process of finding, buying, selling, closing an escrow, and moving is complicated. Having someone by your side as a teammate is imperative. There is an amazing bond that transpires between an agent and their client. You are truly teammates. There are many tasks that are required to accomplish that you will need a teammate who has your back.

Below is a list of a few of the many tasks that are performed:

1. Choosing a buyer
2. Choosing a home
3. Choosing a loan
4. Choosing a sales, offer, and counter offer price
5. Cleaning up credit
6. Creating profit and loss statements
7. Finding a home
8. Fixing up a property
9. Getting proof of income
10. Going over contracts, offers, counter offers, disclosure statements
11. Loan conditions
12. Locating tax returns
13. Meeting appraisers, inspectors, planners, designers, contractors
14. Negotiating contracts
15. Obtaining proof of funds
16. Pulling permits
17. Staging a home
18. Writing letters of explanation

Just like in any team game, you will not win unless you support your teammates. You will not win the game of buying or selling real estate without the support of your agent coach.

Cheerleader

You will have days, moments, and times when you want to give up, times when you want to quit, times when you say to yourself and anyone who might be listening, "I'm tired of this. This game of real estate is not worth it." At these times of frustration you need to have someone in your corner to cheer you up. Your agent is your own private cheerleader. A cheerleader is someone who brings good cheer. When things are not working you need someone to pick you up and encourage you to keep going. Your agent will be there for you.

Sometimes all you may need is someone to listen. Sometimes you need someone who will jump up and down and get you excited. Sometimes you need someone to give you a pep talk. Your agent will do all of these things for you. There are times when you may be having personal problems that have nothing to do with real estate; your agent/ cheerleader will be there for you. When you are in the middle of a troublesome transaction, your agent will be your cheerleader.

COACH

~ a private teacher who gives someone lessons in a particular subject

Source: Merriam-Webster

Accountability Partner

The one great thing about having a coach is that they hold you accountable. Your personal trainer at the gym is a perfect example. You are at the machine at the gym and your personal trainer is standing right there. They instruct you to perform four sets of ten repetitions. They are watching you, counting along with you, looking you in the eye. You have no choice but to do what your trainer has instructed you to do. They are right there to hold you accountable for getting them done.

Your agent is similar to your personal trainer. He or she will give you tasks that will help you to achieve your goals and to assist you in achieving your dreams. They will hold you accountable for completing them. An example is Mrs. Vaughan. I was instructing her in staging her home for sale. This is where you make the home look like a model home to be the most presentable when selling. There is a reason that the builders present or stage their models in the manner that they do. It works. I was instructing Mrs. Vaughan in decluttering her home. I gave her a video to watch. I showed her what an area of her home looked like with the extra chair and how much larger the room looked without the chair. I went to her home three times to help her clear that room and then helped stage the rest of her home to make it look its best.

"The key is not the will to win... everybody has that. It is the will to prepare to win that is important."
~ Bob Knight

> **Fun Fact**
>
> "Success is peace of mind which is a direct result of self-satisfaction in knowing you did your best to become the best you are capable of becoming."
> ~ John Wooden

Spiritual Advisor

I would often hear a buyer who was in the process of looking for a home to buy say, "If it was meant to be, it will be." What they were saying was that the outcome, whether they would get the home or not, was in the hands of the Creator. With all the emotions involved with buying and selling your home, one needs someone who can advise you from a higher or spiritual perspective.

The biggest decisions are, "Do I sell or buy at this time?" Your agent will not make this decision for you. Your agent will hold the space for you to make these decisions yourself. Holding the space could simply be listening and repeating back what was said. It could be gathering information or talking. Your agent will listen to your concerns and often simply to allow you to talk it out. Often when given space and opportunity to simply talk, you can easily making these critical decisions.

One of my favorite clients was Mrs. McCarthy. Mrs. McCarthy was a widow in her mid eighties; she loved her home. She also had a desire to be closer to her children and grandchildren. There was also a concern to have a smaller place with less upkeep. All I did was take the time out of my day and sit with Mrs. McCarthy for about an hour one Friday morning. She talked about her kids and grandchildren. She shared about family gatherings that took place in her home. And at the end of about an hour and five minutes, Mrs. McCarthy made the decision to move. I had held the space for her to choose what was best for her. For an hour I was her spiritual advisor.

Teacher

Real estate, like most professions, has its own specialized vocabulary or lingo. I'll never forget Jenny Hobson, who laughed when she stated, "David, soon with your teaching I'll have this real estate lingo down." Jenny was saying that I was teaching her the language that was specific to real estate.

Your agent will be your teacher in more than the terms and specific language of real estate. He or she will teach you about loans, trends, neighborhoods, inspections, home designs, prices, schools, traffic flow, heating and air-conditioning systems, and much more.

Passion

There are times in anything you do that you get tired, discouraged, and resigned. Your agent will bring passion to your real estate transactions to make sure that you don't give up. When things don't go as planned it's almost natural to lose passion. At times it seems easier to quit. Real estate can be hard with all the problems that come up. When you are buying there are loan conditions, property conditions, and seemingly endless issues that come one after another.

The former Vise President Hubert H. Humphrey said, "Never give in and never give up." It takes passion from your agent to deal with all the issues associate in real estate. It would be ordinary or reasonable to quit. Your agent has the passion to not give in and to never give up. Just like Hubert H. Humphrey, your agent will not give up on you.

> "A common mistake among those who work in sport is spending a disproportional amount of time on "x's and o's" as compared to time spent learning about people."
> ~ Mike Krzyzewski

Compassion

You will also need someone to show you compassion. We are only human and thus we have flaws. We make mistakes and we often do things or not do things we later regret. Your agent has compassion for you and your missteps, imperfections, mistakes, and flaws.

I remember when I bought my first home. I was only twenty-one years old and scared. I was afraid of making a mistake. I was afraid I would get cheated or swindled. Out of my fear, I missed and was late to several appointments. My agent never got angry or upset with me. I'll never forget Charleen.

Charleen took me aside and talked to me. She gave me the space to express my fears. She took the time and gifted me with the compassion I needed to express what I needed to say. Charleen drove me to see all the comparable properties. She showed me the market trends and explained the history of the neighborhood. She explained the possibilities as well as the potential pitfalls. With the information and compassion Charleen provided I was able to move forward to buy my first property. Charleen gave me my first glimpse into what it takes to be a real estate agent.

"A coach's greatest asset is his sense of responsibility - the reliance placed on him by his players."
~ Knute Rockne

Love

To be your real estate agent there has to be love. An agent has a love for real estate and a love for what they are doing. There is an old saying credited to Marc Anthony, "If you do what you love, you'll never work a day in your life." Your agent loves the art of real estate. To fully comprehend and appreciate the *101 reasons to love your real estate agent* is the point of this book. Weaving all of these tasks and ways of being together is an art. To be a true artist one must love what they do.

Real estate isn't a full-time job; it is more like a full-time job times two. I found you can't do it part-time. Your agent is on call and on the job 24/7/365; there isn't a day off. There is always something to get done, someone to call, a problem to solve. If one is going to take on being a real estate agent, there must be love.

Your real estate agent can work a sixteen-hour day and not know it. He or she could forget to eat. They love their work so much that time stops. To say that your agent loves you as their client is not an inaccurate statement. Without you, your agent doesn't have an opportunity to do what they love.

Conclusion

Everyone can use a coach. Even Michael Jordan, the greatest basketball player of all time, had a coach. If Michael had a coach as great as he was, it would be reasonable that everyone could benefit from a coach. Your agent, with all of their other duties, will coach you through all of your real estate transactions and teach you the art of real estate. Your agent acts as your coach as they guide you through your real estate transactions. They will guide you, teach you, educate you, and cheer you on.

Recap - Coach

Teammate: someone who works directly with you to achieve a mutual agreed-upon goal.

Cheerleader: a person who encourages and inspires you to perform at a higher level than you thought possible.

Accountability Partner: a person who will check on you to make sure you are moving in the direction of your goals and dreams.

Spiritual Advisor: one who offers possible solutions in areas of life, someone who guides someone on their journey through life's ups and downs.

Teacher: a instructor or tutor to give you information and ways of being regarding real estate.

Passion: the ability to be excited and stay excited.

Compassion: understanding and conveying concern regarding someone's situation.

Love: the ability to be fully engaged and continually excited, with affinity in what one is doing and who they are.

XII. Marketing Executive

"The aim of marketing is to know and understand the customer so well the product or service fits him and sells itself."

~ Peter Drucker
Management consultant, educator, and author

There are many hats that your agent wears. Another job that is extremely important is the one of marketing executive. Marketing and selling property can be considered the top item on your agent's to do list.

It is no small thing to complete all of the tasks involved in marketing a property. Your agent will design ads, write the content, and then distribute them in a cornucopia of methods. Some of the methods your agent utilizes to market property are print, Internet, radio, television, YouTube, neighborhood, agents, websites, and more. Your agent is your private marketing executive.

Planner

Before your real estate agent or any marketing executive does anything, they must plan. You may have heard of the saying, "Before you go on vacation you have to first know where it is you want to go." Zig Ziglar wrote, "Many people spend more time in planning the wedding than they do in planning the marriage." Planning is extremely important. If you decide you want to visit Chicago you have to figure out how to get there.

Known as the greatest coach of all time, John Wooden planned for two hours for every one hour of his UCLA team's practices. Being busy isn't planning. Thomas Edison stated, "Being busy does not always mean real work. The object of all work is production or accomplishment, and to either of these ends there must be forethought, system planning, intelligence, and honest purpose as well as perspiration." Your agent has to determine what will be most effective for each particular task or job and make a plan that corresponds with determination.

Ad Designer

Once your agent makes a plan, he or she will design an ad to attract a buyer or seller. Designing an advertisement to market and sell a property or to attract a seller is no small thing. There is a lot of knowledge, skill, and creativity that goes into designing an effective ad. Your agent is required to acquire these skills as another task to be of assistance to you.

When you stop to think about it, there are countless methods, ideas, and ways an ad can be created. Your real estate agent will create advertisements that are unique and one of a kind to fit a specific property.

Ad Writer

Your agent will also write your advertisements. He or she will be diligent in finding the best words, phrases, features, and benefits of a property to best demonstrate a property's value. There is an art to the craft of writing an ad that will make the phone ring. I remember I resisted learning how to write an effective ad. I thought that I was writing a bunch of hyperbole. I found that it took creativity to attract a buyer. I began to think of ad writing as a creative art. I reframed my thinking and considered how to best describe a property in such a way as to describe its features in an expressive, vibrant, and colorful manner.

Marketing

~ the activities that are involved in making people aware of a company's products, making sure that the products are available to be bought, etc.

Source: Merriam-Webster

Print

Your agent is an expert at print advertising. Print advertising is any advertising that is printed. This includes newspapers, magazines, direct mail, billboards, posters, and even the benches on bus stops are print ads. It is true that print advertising isn't as prominent as it once was, but it is still an important skill that your agent has in his or her bag of skills.

Print ads have been one of the major methods a real estate agent uses to locate buyers to buy property.

Your agent is skilled in:

1.   determining what type of ads will be most effective
2.   how to best write them
3.   in what medium
4.   what graphics and pictures will be most effective
5.   when to place the ads.

It is easy to see how knowledge and expertise in the skill of print advertising is critical.

Fun Fact

~ "Casual Friday" is the product of a guerrilla marketing campaign by Levis' new khaki brand, Dockers, during the early 90's recession.

Source: marketplace.org

Internet

The Internet, or online advertising, also called online marketing or web advertising, is a form of marketing and advertising which uses the Internet to deliver promotional marketing messages to buyers and sellers. It includes email, search engine marketing (SEM), and social media marketing, many types of display advertising (including web banner advertising), and mobile advertising. Internet marketing is an entire field of expertise on its own.

Radio

Radio isn't used as often as other forms of advertising. However, it is another skill your agent has to market your property. Now that radio is also online it is more of a possibility for a consumer to have access to it. Your agent can be creative and take a radio spot that was recorded and place that clip on their website or within another online advertisement. This can only give credibility to the ad and the property you are selling, it can offer a unique method of displaying it.

"Don't blame the marketing department. The buck stops with the chief executive."
~ John D. Rockefeller

Television

Television is another method to attract a buyer or a seller. With the local television, cable, and online television, there are more opportunities than ever to display a property on screen, whether it is your computer or television. And just like with a radio advertisement, a television advertisement is a creative method to show off the features of a property, and the clip can be utilized in many different ways to capture the flavor of a particular property.

YouTube

YouTube is an amazing marketing tool. YouTube is a storage place and a launching pad for videos of property. You can use it as a link for a website. It can be used in an email campaign, and it will create expose directly from the YouTube site.

A YouTube video can be illustrated by the quote often attributed to Napoléon Bonaparte: "A picture is worth a thousand words." I believe it was one of my mentors, the 2001 champion of public speaking Darren LaCroix, who laminated the idea by saying, "A video is worth a thousand pictures." Wow, that would be a thousand times a thousand. Darren is saying a video is as valuable or impactful as a million words.

When you make a video of a property, it comes alive. At the writing of this chapter, there is a technology where a picture becomes a small clip of a video. The picture comes alive. This is what a property does when made into a video. To be fair and complete, there are other methods and places to store and share your videos. I'm using YouTube as the example as it is the most widely known and used platform for this type of usage at the time of this writing. The point is you have a medium that rocks and is effective. We will go into the skills necessary to be a producer of the videos in the next chapter.

Neighborhood

The old-fashioned method of obtaining clients is to canvas, or door knock, around a neighborhood. Your agent will do this by physically knocking on doors. The concept is that the homeowner in a neighborhood might know someone who they would like to have as a new neighbor. They might also know of a neighbor who is considering or planning on moving. People who are renting in a particular neighborhood may want to buy a property in that neighborhood.

Your agent will also be going door-to-door looking for people to sell their home. They are looking for a home for you to buy, a home in a neighborhood that you already are interested in.

"There was a period of time in America where the advertising world actually went to the housewives of America and had them write jingles that would appeal to them. It was actually brilliant marketing."
~ Julianne Moore

Email Campaigns

Your agent has a list of potential buyers, sellers, past clients, family, and friends who he or she will distribute information to via email. Your agent will design mailings to generate clients to buy your property as part of an overall marking campaign. They will track and refine their mailings based on what works and doesn't work.

Another method your agent will put to work for you is to market other agents via email. There is a rule in life that is also true in real estate; 20% of the agents sell 80% of the properties. This phenomenon is known as the 80/20 rule.

Knowing the 80/20 rule I would mail a flyer of the properties that I was marketing for sale to the 20% of the local agents who did 80% of the sales. Note: This was before there was such a thing as email, so I was forced to do a physical mailing. There are many different email campaign systems that one can utilize to distribute information regarding a property. Now it is possible to do these mailing with a click of a mouse via email.

Physical Mail

Physical mailings are still effective. There is something about being able to hold and touch a piece of mail. Postcards are also great for mailing. The receiver, whether an agent or potential client, doesn't have to open an envelope. With a postcard they can hold and immediately see the information. Pictures are effective in getting the reader's attention and relaying the message. Again, your agent is an expert in determining the design, layout, and content of the physical mailings to agents, clients, and prospects.

Website

A good functional, creative, and interactive website is just another activity that your agent does to assist you. Your agent will either hire or be the webmaster for their website that will benefit you. They will be posting a listing, (pictures and descriptions) of your property. If you are a buyer their website will be interactive where you will be able to access information about properties, how to qualify, and information about loans, property, real estate trends, laws, and anything real estate-related.

Blog

Your agent can write a blog about real estate, the local area, real estate financing, market trends, real estate law, and more. Your property can be featured in a blog as another method for gaining exposure. Writing a blog is another of the many diverse skills your real estate agent utilizes to assist you in achieving your real estate goals.

> "People are in such a hurry to launch their product or business that they seldom look at marketing from a bird's eye view and they don't create a systematic plan."
> ~ Dave Ramsey

Social Media

Facebook, Twitter, Instagram, and Linked-In are a few of the social media tools that your agent utilizes for you. Social media provides global access to your property. It is also another method for your agent to locate properties you may be interested in. Social media is just another tool your agent utilizes for you.

Conclusion

When you hire a real estate agent you hire a marketing executive. A marketing executive makes many choices, such as what, when, where, how and how much advertising to do. Your agent has acquired all the skills necessary to be an effective marketing executive.

Recap - Marketing Executive

Planner: choosing the what, when, where, how and how much, to do or not to do something.

Ad Design: the creation of all the designs and scheme arrangements of an ad.

Ad Writer: writing anything that is in print or spoken for an advertisement.

Print: any and all types and aspects of ads that are physically printed.

Internet: an advertisement that goes out through the Internet.

Radio: there are still radio ads and interviews your agent

can give to market and
locate buyers and sellers.

Television: your agent can utilize
local and cable television.

YouTube: a storage and launching
pad for videos.

Neighborhood: canvassing door-to-door
in targeted areas is
effective.

Email Campaigns: a periodic email
marketing campaign is
cost-effective and an
efficient marketing
strategy.

Physical Mail: a well-planned, produced,
and printed piece of marketing
material can touch a prospect
physically and emotionally.

Website: your property will be
displayed on your agent's
website.

Blog: a periodic written, or
video your agent uses to
inform the viewer, or listener,
about real estate.

Social Media: methods your agent utilizes to
expose a property for you and
also to find a property you
may be looking for.

XIII. Producer

"Being busy does not always mean real work. The object of all work is production or accomplishment, and to either of these ends, there must be forethought, system planning, intelligence, and honest purpose, as well as perspiration. Seeming to do is not doing."

~ Thomas A. Edison
Inventor

Your agent is also a movie producer. That's right, in order to take pictures and videos of your property your agent has the skills of a movie producer. Videos that appear on YouTube, websites, social media, and all over the Internet don't make themselves. Your real estate agent has the talent to create these mini-masterpieces. The following is just a rundown of some of the skills your agent performs as a producer.

Director

The duties of director for your agent can be thought of similarly to a director in a movie. As a director your agent coordinates the project or video: what the video is to feature; the who, what, when, where, how, and why of the video. Then your agent will direct how to set up the shot, what will be featured, and the overall scope and purpose of the video.

"I thought Star Wars was too wacky for the general public."
~ George Lucas

Writer

There must be a plan to what the video is intended to accomplish. Even if it isn't formally written, there is a plan in the mind of your agent. In the videos I have been making lately I write out an outline of what I want to say. This way I have a general idea of what I want to accomplish in the video. I have, in essence, written a script for the video. Your agent will do the same for the videos they create for you.

Concept Design

Your real estate agent will design a concept for the piece they are working on. Your agent will create an idea of what they want to convey to the potential buyers and sellers. It isn't any different than that of a real movie producer. A producer may decide to make a movie about the real West and what it was like to be an authentic cowboy or cowgirl. Your agent may decide that they want the viewer to get an experience of the community that a property is located in. In another, they may want to capture the fact that a home is most suited to children because of the pool and the four bedrooms.

It is the same as it is in goal setting. The producer needs to know exactly where they want to go or what they want to accomplish in order to arrive there. Designing a concept is how your agent will begin the process of producing a video for a property.

Producer

~ a person who supervises or finances a work (as a staged or recorded performance) for exhibition or dissemination to the public

Source: Merriam-Webster

Staging

We talked about staging a property for sale in chapter two. You also want to stage a home to film a video. To review: staging is making a property look and feel its best. If you have ever seen a model home that a builder provides to show buyers, this is how a staged home will look. A model home is a classic example of staging, color, clean and clutter as the basics. Your agent will make sure the colors go together and are pleasing and appropriate for each room of the home.

A staged home is perfectly cleaned and all the clutter has been removed. There is a remarkable and noticeable difference when a home is clean and the clutter has been removed. An example you can use for yourself regarding staging is your desk or the top of your dresser. Notice your desk and dresser with ten or fifteen items on it, and then remove most all of the items and notice how it looks and feels. There is a physiological feeling that occurs when things are clean and free of clutter.

> "So that's the dissenter's hope: that they are writing not for today but for tomorrow."
> ~ Ruth Bader Ginsburg

Production Designer

A production designer is someone who gets everything ready to film the video. There are a lot of things to consider. One is the blocking of the scene or property. This could be making sure there are children playing in the pool, a cat is lying on the couch, or there is food cooking in the kitchen. To display the property in its best light your agent will do the necessary things to get ready to film a property.

Lighting

Lighting is extremely important in filming anything. There is a reason we have the expression, "to see it in the best light." For a picture to be worth a thousand words, and for a movie to be worth a thousand pictures, one must be able to clearly see what is being filmed. I film a blog every week and have several lights that I use in order to be seen clearly. Your agent will make sure all lights are on, all drapes are open, and the filming is done when there is the most light. Your agent as a producer will arrange the lighting to make sure that your property is, "seen in its best light."

> "The production of too many useful things results in too many useless people."
> ~ Karl Marx

Photographer

In this chapter I have focused on videos. However, there are times that a still shot is necessary and effective in marketing a property. This section shows what your real estate agent does for you while wearing the hat of a photographer.

A property doesn't take pictures of itself. There is a lot more to taking a picture than pointing and clicking. Here is a list of some of the techniques your agent uses in displaying and showing off your property, as explained by Jim Miotke and betterphoto.com.

1. Move in closer to the subject of the picture. This helps the viewer understand what the picture is about.
2. Compose the picture with care by:
    a. Keeping the horizon in line
    b. Cropping out elements that are not necessary
    c. Playing with perspective so that all lines show a pattern or lead the eye to your main subject
    d. Rule of thirds…have the subject off center to create interest and contrast
3. Be Selective. Watch the borders of your picture to make sure there isn't anything distracting from that main subject. For instance, if you are focusing on the kitchen cabinets, move the toaster out of the way.
4. Watch the lighting. When filming outside, it is best to have the sun behind you. Again, turn on all the lights and open all the drapes when inside.
5. A more advanced tip is to play with focus. When you focus on the subject of the picture and thus defocus on the rest of the picture, you create a dynamic shot. An example would be a picture where the fireplace is in focus and the rest of the picture is not. That will create a dynamic picture, putting the attention on a featured subject, the fireplace.

With the new technology, photos can be edited, cropped, and arranged in many different ways. Your agent will take time, energy, and expertise in making each and every photo look its best in representing your property.

Videographer

Like taking photographs, there is more to being a videographer than pointing and clicking. Similar to taking photographs, your agent must be aware of the lighting, the background, and staging of the property. To capture the features of a property, your agent as a videographer will take wide, medium, and close-up views of the unique features of your property. They will be aware of what is in the background as to feature the aspect they are focusing on. They will frame the shot like a picture. They will also use the rule of thirds.

FUN FACT !

Fun Fact

"Busyness is not a reason for not getting other things done. It is an excuse for not claiming your true priorities."

~ Alan Cohen

Where being a videographer differs is in the sound. There are different options regarding adding sounds. One option is to simply explain to the viewer what they are looking at. Your agent will not be doing too much of, "This is the living room," as you can clearly see that it is the living room. They will explain some features that are not readily known in the viewing, such as the type of wood used in the crown molding. Another quality that can add to the sound is music. There is something soothing and inviting about music. The right selection could make the difference in a sale.

There are a plethora of options when editing a video. As stated above, there are the options of adding music, what to cut, what to include, and what to add. One can shoot the same scene ten times and take portions of each one. You can add and mix still shots in with your video. You can add captions and explanations. Your agent can and will create a masterpiece for you.

Mastering

Mastering can be something that takes on an effect all its own. This includes the sound and film (digital) editing. The adding of transitions between scenes, titles, and backgrounds are all choices your real estate agent makes as the producer of your videos and stills that are created for you. The mastering includes editing and finishing the project to show your property in its best light.

> **"I always say I make pictures rather than take pictures."**
> **~ Terry Richardson**

Distribution

This is where your real estate agent will place the piece once it is completed. Some of the obvious places are websites, Facebook, blogs, Instagram, YouTube, Google, local television ads, and more.

Conclusion

The entire purpose of this book is to demonstrate the value of your real estate agent for you. Being a producer is just one more of the many facets or hats that your agent possesses for you. Producing a media piece is an artistic endeavor that needs to be recognized. Just like the creation of a painting by Rembrandt, they don't happen by themselves. There is time, effort, and talent involved, all provided by your real estate agent.

Recap - Producer

Director:	the conductor of a project.
Writer:	the creator of the dialogue or way a piece is to be written.
Concept Design:	how the project is to be created and put together.
Staging:	the placement and the physical design of how the shot is arranged.
Production Designer:	the process of actually getting all the equipment arranged and the shooting,
Lighting:	ensuring proper and adequate lighting for a shot.
Photographer:	taking still shots, or pictures.

Videographer: taking moving shots, or videos.

Mastering: putting the piece together, the film, sound, transitions, titles, background, mixing, editing, and finishing.

Distribution: all of the outlets where the project is placed.

XIV. Problem Solver

"We cannot solve our problems with the same level of thinking that created them."

~ Albert Einstein
Theoretical Physicist

Problems are built into real estate. The single reason your real estate agent gets paid and is worth making a great living is their ability to solve problems. This chapter goes into many of the methods your agent utilizes to solve the many problems that are inherent in real estate.

Most all sellers are invested in getting the absolute highest price for their properties, and to close on time. Sellers, in general, want their buyers to buy their properties, "as is," without any complaints, at or above the asking price. A seller wants everyone to take care of everything before they even know there was something that needed to be done.

The buyer in a typical real estate transaction wants the lowest price possible. A quintessential buyer wants every single aspect and feature of a property to be in perfect working order, pristine, and for everything to be or at least look brand new. The buyer wants to get everything done including the closing date when it is most convenient for them and their family.

The tradesmen and women who may be working on a property want to be able to get things done on their schedules. They want to fit a job around their other projects and personal lives. They want to make the most money possible, with the least amount of effort and problems.

Many loan representatives want to make as much money as fast as possible. They want to make a loan and get it funded ASAP. If it is the end of the month they want to get it funded in that month. They are also interested in taking care of their client and getting everything done before the rates go up or someone changes their mind. Some loan representatives are working on many loans at a time. They may have higher-priority loans, be too busy, understaffed, or unorganized, thus delaying the closing date.

The loan underwriter wants to be absolutely sure that the buyer can afford the property. They ask for everything they can think of to ensure they have all of the data to show they were diligent in their job. They make sure they have every detail covered to prove that the buyer can afford the property. The underwriter wants to be assured the buyer can indeed afford and be able to repay the loan without going into default.

The two agents, (buyer's agent and seller's agent), want what's best for their client and also themselves. They want to get paid. They want their client to get the best deal and close on schedule. The agent's goals, timetables, and agendas are rarely the same. With all these conflicting agendas one can clearly understand that problem solving would indeed be a major asset.

Deal Keeper

In my opinion, the ability to keep a deal or to close the transaction is the most important skill your agent can possess. In my real estate career, I have seen dozens of transactions canceled needlessly because the agent lacked these skills.

There was an agent in my office named Alice. Alice was working with a cute older couple who were excited to be moving from Ohio to California. They were moving to live near their children who were professors at the Claremont colleges. They were thrilled to be moving to the great weather and to be near their children and grandchildren.

> "If I had an hour to solve a problem I'd spend 55 minutes thinking about the problem and 5 minutes thinking about solutions."
> ~ Albert Einstein

The escrow had some problems because the property was considered a historical home. The home needed a new roof, and because it was a historical property, the roof couldn't be replaced by installing an affordable composition roof. The roof had to be Spanish tile as it was originally in 1909.

The seller agreed to pay for a cheaper composition roof, but not the price of a Spanish tile roof, which was over triple the price. The couple and the seller couldn't agree on how to pay the difference between the costs of the cheaper and more expensive roofs. Rather than sticking in there and finding a solution to the problem, Alice quit. She canceled everything and simply walked away from the transaction and the older couple.

"Never bring the problem-solving stage into the decision-making stage. Otherwise, you surrender yourself to the problem rather than the solution."
~ Robert H. Schuller

As it turned out, our office manager Ken stepped in and handled the problem. Our office made less than half of the commission as originally agreed upon, and it took an additional three months to close. When all was done the sellers were happy, the property remained a historical property for the city, and most of all, the older couple could not have been happier.

Connector

What I mean by connector is someone who can put different people together, one who knows the best contractor, handyman, painter, plumber, and so on. An agent has the connections and ability to find and make friends with the people to help make your life easier. Knowing the best and most reasonable craftsmen can make all the difference in a real estate transaction.

There was a house that was located on a slope, built before there were any regulations on building safety. The lender wouldn't give a loan for this property due to the slope. The buyer wanted to buy. The seller wanted to sell. I happened to know Jim, who had a backhoe, which was the perfect piece of equipment to adjust the slope to fit the city regulations. Jim spent a weekend adjusting the slope to satisfy the city's regulations. Then working with Jim, we brought in my friend Eddie to build a retaining wall. The transaction closed, the buyer, the seller, and city were all happy. Without my connections with Jim and Eddie, who adjusted the slope and built the retaining wall, the transaction would not have been possible.

A connector is also an attribute to aide in being a negotiator. A negotiator is one who settles issues of price, closing dates, items included, and excluded in a sale. Your real estate agent has the ability to connect people within the negotiating process. They make negotiations easier, more effective, and often possible at times when they would seem impossible. An example would be simply the ability and willingness to make friends with the other agent and even the buyer and seller. People will be more willing to make compromises with someone whom they like, know, and with whom they have built rapport.

As mentioned above in the section, *Deal Keeper*, every real estate transaction can be easier when there is a connection. In every transaction, there is a price and terms that needs to be decided. The buyer wants the lowest price and the best terms for themselves, and the seller wants the highest price and the most favorable terms for themselves. When your agent makes a connection with all the personalities in a transaction, your life is easier, more peaceful with more freedom from anxiety and stress.

Solve

~ to find a way to deal with and end (a problem)

~ to find the correct answer to (something, such as a riddle)

~ to find the correct explanation for (something, such as a mystery)

Source: Merriam-Webster

Peacemaker

A peacemaker is someone who does just that, makes the peace. If you have been part of a real estate transaction, been in a business partnership or a romantic relationship you know that there are times when there is a need to make peace. Your agent is a person who can see and understand all sides of a situation. Your agent is on your side with a fiduciary duty to you. They have a clear perspective of all sides giving them the ability to make peace. There are times when it seems there is no other way out than to cancel the transaction and forget the whole thing. Your agent has the expertise, experience, and know-how to settle even the most difficult situations.

Psychologist

Real estate can be hard when one side of a transaction wants one thing and the other side wants something else. There seems to be no middle ground. There can be a lot involved: kids, schools, packing, movers, days off work, repairs, painting, new flooring, and decorating. In the middle of a real estate transaction, your plans can blow up in a matter of seconds.

My friend Keith Hanson's son Kevin was about to enter medical school. This wasn't just any medical school; this was Harvard medical school. He and his family had everything arranged, and they went so far as to put their rental home on the market to have the funds to buy a home in Cambridge for Kevin to live in for the six years he expected to be in medical school. Everything was going perfectly until the buyer for the rental home lost his job just two weeks before escrow was due to close and three weeks prior to Kevin's first class at Harvard.

You can see that Mr. and Mrs. Hanson, as well as Kevin, needed someone to hear their problems. I immediately went to work to get another buyer for the rental home. This event required Kevin to rent an apartment for two and a half months and move twice. This cost a lot of time Kevin could have been working on his studies. In addition, Kevin had to miss several classes. There were additional costs of the apartment, moving twice, and storage fees. In addition, the Hanson's ended up selling the rental home for $6,000 less to the new buyer. This situation required me to fill the role of a psychologist and simply allow the Hanson's to express their frustrations.

Inventor

The ability to solve problems is imperative when working in real estate. There are almost always problems. If your real estate agent is the type who gives up and walks away at the first sign of trouble, they are not your agent. Your true agent will be an inventor when it comes to figuring out and fighting for a method to get your transactions closed. This Ralph Waldo Emerson quote says it all, "Every wall is a door." is appropriate for your agent for life. They only see possibilities, he or she will never stop trying, and never stop inventing a way when there appears to be no way to be of service.

**"A problem well put is
half solved."
~ John Dewey**

Jack of all Trades

Your agent will be someone who can do just about anything that it takes to complete a transaction. Someone who can make things happen, when for most anyone else it wasn't going to. Jack of all trades, means just that; your agent will use any legal means to get you what you want. Your agent utilizes creativity, resourcefulness, and cunning with the tenacity to never give up to close even the most difficult transactions.

In chapter nine Salesmanship, under the topic problem solver, I shared about Edward and Teresa Logan who had a problem. At the outset, it seemed like a deal breaker. The Logans were moving from a small home in San Dimas to a home that the back yard was next to the Glendora County Club golf course. This was not a step up; it was two maybe three. The Logans were happy to find such a great home that they could live in for the rest of their lives. Then Teresa noticed that the home had an unusually large overhang on the eaves. This was a home built in the late '70s; the architect and builder gave the home a modern look. The problem was that the Logans had a motor home that they wanted to park in the rear of the home where there was a perfect spot next to the garage to park it. However, the overhang made it impossible to get the motorhome from the front to the back without hitting the overhang.

This is where I became a jack of all trades. The old saying, "It's not what you know but who you know," came into play. I played badminton with a local architect, and there was a contractor who was in and out of the office almost every day. I considered both Jack and Mike to be my friends. I arranged a meeting with Jack the architect, Mike the contractor, the Logans, the seller, and the seller's agent.

Jack said that cutting off three feet of the overhang wouldn't detract from the looks functionally nor the ascetics of the property. Then Mike gave an estimate of the cost to cut off three feet of the eave to make room for the motorhome to fit in and out of the driveway. This all went well, everyone was happy, and the transaction was able to close.

This is a perfect example of a Jack of all trades. There is no definite job description or task. It is the willingness and ability to get it done, to be a cause in the matter and make things happen. Your agent for life is a jack of all trades.

"When written in Chinese, the word 'crisis' is composed of two characters. One represents danger and the other represents opportunity."
~ John F. Kennedy

Resource

Your agent is a resource for information, information to solve your problems. Your agent can tap into their vast warehouse of experience. They will go back in their mind to a similar problem that they experienced or may have known about. Your agent will remember how that problem was solved and will immediately implement a solution.

Your agent also has vast problem-solving resources available to them. They have their entire office with a broker and the owner whom they can brainstorm with to generate solutions. Your agent has access to lawyers from the national, state, and local Associations of Realtors. If your agent works for a large company, most of them have their own lawyers and experts that they have access to.

Your agent also has a vast network of professionals and associates in many various professions, occupations, and trades whom he or she can consult on your behalf. In short, your agent has a plethora of reassures to ensure your success.

> ### Fun Fact
>
> "Problems are not stop signs, they are guidelines."
>
> ~ Robert H. Schuller

Inductive Reasoning

Inductive reasoning is the scientific method. Your agent takes situations or problems she or he has observed in the past and determines hypotheses or steps to solve problems. Then your agent designed a way to test the steps. Did the steps work or not? Then the process to solve a particular problem is proven by repeating the process of solving that particular problem. Much of the reasoning performed by your agent is intuitive and automatic based on past experience, and he or she will utilize inductive reasoning based on their past success.

Fortune Teller

Your agent acts like a fortuneteller. They can often see what could go wrong before anything does go wrong. Your real estate agent looks at what could go amiss. Sometimes it's not really that hard to do. You don't need any superhuman skills or the ability to see into the future. You can often see it if you take the time and have the guts to look.

An example was Eddie. Eddie was a buyer for a duplex I had for sale. He was a very nice person, polite, well-dressed, and a bit of a people pleaser. Eddie did what was expected of him and didn't seem to have the ability to say no. I felt an inauthenticity about Eddie from the start. He was just too easy to deal with. Eddie was buying the property to have his grandmother live in the front house, and he was going to live in the smaller back house. I also noticed that Eddie was constantly late for our appointments. I could see and feel from the start that this wasn't something he really wanted to do.

Later I found out that Eddie wanted to move to Florida, where his girlfriend lived. The arrangement with his grandmother was his mother's idea. Eddie just didn't have the guts to say no. I didn't know this information up front, but there were signs. For one, Eddie didn't make any decision without his mother's approval. This was a red flag because his mother was not on the loan and wasn't going to live there. Another clue was that Eddie accepted the property "as is." A duplex normally has more issues than a single-family home, and most buyers who would be living there would want the property brought up to standards. As it turned out, Eddie backed out of the deal on the fifty-eighth day of the sixty-day escrow.

> "Most people spend more time and energy going around problems than in trying to solve them."
> ~ Henry Ford

In hindsight, it was easy to see that this was likely to occur. Any good fortuneteller could see. And remember, if you are dealing with an average real estate agent, they will be blinded by their future paycheck and not be at all interested in saving you the fifty-eight days plus that an Eddie will cost you. Here are the signs that it wouldn't take a fortuneteller to see:

1. Eddie had a girlfriend in Florida.
2. Eddie was going to live in the smaller house in the back.
3. His mother was consulted for every detail.
4. He was a people pleaser and rarely said no.
5. He was often late showing up for appointments.

Your agent will look, be aware of, see, note, and take action on problems before they become one. In this case, it would have been easy to take Eddie aside and have a talk with him, get to the truth, and avoid the headache and heartache of an escrow canceling at the last minute.

Conclusion

The skill to problem solve, in my opinion, is one of the most important qualities of your agent for life. This is why they get paid the big bucks. Without this skill, they wouldn't get paid at all because the transactions wouldn't close. You wouldn't wind up buying or selling your home without an agent who could solve problems.

Problems are inherent when there are two parties who want different things. Your agent not only has a bag of tricks to refer to, he or she is the problem solver who gets things done. Your agent has the skill to understand both sides of a transaction, to see what each party wants to accomplish, and to determine what is fair and correct in each situation.

I had a transaction where the roof was obviously worn and the buyer was willing to buy the property and accept the roof in its current condition. The problem occurred when the appraiser called for the roof to be replaced. One might think that this is totally the seller's responsibility. The appraiser did say it needed to be replaced; however, the buyer and seller had already come to an agreement with the roof the way it was.

Everyone knew it was a roof with only a few years of life left. Knowing this, the seller took the roof condition into account and adjusted the price. The buyer accepted the property and price with the roof in "as is" condition. Some might think that the buyer should be the one to pay for the roof. It may sound simple to simply go 50% each. However, both parties wanted the other party to pay 100% for the roof. It took me almost three weeks to convince both sides to fully understand the dynamics of the situation to the point where they both compromised and were happy to do so, and thus solve the problem.

Your agent for life will solve most all your real estate problems and often some of your problems that aren't even real estate-related. They will get things done and make your life easier.

Recap - Problem Solver

Deal Keeper:

someone who makes things happen...no matter what.

Connector:

the ability to put agents, tradesman, associates, and others together.

Peacemaker:

the skill to settle people down and see common ground.

Psychologist:

someone who can listen and understand what another is going through.

Inventor:

figuring out a solution when there appears to be none.

Jack of All Trades:

producing a wide variety of actions to solve a problem.

Resource: having a wealth of knowledge to draw from to cause a solution.

Inductive Reasoning: a method of creating probable solutions and testing them by one's experience.

Fortune Teller: your agent's ability to see a potential problem before it happens and take steps to prevent it.

XV. Information & Design Technologist

"I just invent, then wait until man comes around to needing what I've invented."

~ R. Buckminster Fuller
Architect, author, designer, & inventor

There are so many tasks that your agent manages for you, it's difficult to imagine someone who can do so much. Another entire field that your real estate agent for life has mastered to be of service to you is the field of information and design technologist. Each and every section of this chapter has its own and unique skill set and is a career of its own.

Data Entry

Data entry is a task that is carried out by your real estate agent most every day. The data includes the information in fliers, advertising, the multiple listing service, lists of past and future clients, agents, and affiliates. Data entry is involved when you are a buyer looking for a property. The details of the property you are looking for must be entered into the search application to perform a property search. Your agent also imports the data of the most capable agents who may have buyers for your property when you are selling.

It may sound like an easy task and that anyone can do it. And when you look at all the different websites and systems that your agent must navigate to perform the data entry, you will discover that there is a lot more to it than one would imagine.

Technology

~ the use of science in industry, engineering, etc., to invent useful things or to solve problems

~ a machine, piece of equipment, method, etc., that is created by technology

Source: Merriam-Webster

Database Manager

There is also more to data entry than putting the information into a database. The data must be managed. Managing data can be a laborious task. Database management is a lot like balancing your checkbook or doing dishes after every usage. It's easier to simply input information and forget about it. You can imagine what happens to something when you just forget about it. It was like how my room was as a kid-a mess. The details must be managed to be properly utilized.

Properties go on and off the market. Agents retire, change careers, or move to another area. Buyers and sellers buy and sell and therefore are no longer in the market.

There is an old saying, "The only constant is change," and as things change in a database they must be kept up-to-date to remain viable and usable. Data kept up-to-date will be more effective for you in buying or selling your most important asset you may ever have, namely your home.

Appraiser

Most agents are not actual real estate appraisers, and your agent is an expert in the field of real estate appraisal. In fact, estimating value is almost a daily function for your real estate agent. A real estate appraiser is one who estimates the value of real estate. Estimating value is done by gathering and analyzing data of properties that are similar to the property that one is evaluating.

There are five categories that are analyzed:

1. properties that are currently on the market (active)
2. properties that have sold and closed escrow (sold)
3. properties that have sold and have yet to close escrow (pending)
4. properties on the market or pending that were canceled (canceled)
5. properties that never sold (expired)

Your agent will find properties that are most like the subject property and analyze and compare them to the subject, putting the most credence on the similar properties that have recently sold and closed escrow. (Properties that sold six months or more prior to the time of the estimate may be representing a completely different market and are considered to a lesser degree). Your agent gives less weight to the other four categories in determining value. Your agent will then add or subtract for features each property has or doesn't have in comparison to the subject property. In other words if everything is the same and the comparable property has a pool and the subject does not, there will be a subtraction of value for the subject property.

The art of real estate appraisal is a complete and important job on its own. For example, when you are selling your home and your agent determines the value to be lower than the actual value, it will cost you money. If the estimate is too high and doesn't sell, an incorrect estimate of value will cost you time. Your agent has the expertise, the experience, and ability to skillfully offer an accurate estimate of value for most any property. If you have not realized by now, your agent truly has earned the right to be your agent for life.

> **"It's not a faith in technology.**
> **It's faith in people."**
> **~ Steve Jobs**

Graphic Designer

I didn't even know there was such a term as graphic designer when I was creating flyers for my sellers back in 1986. The term at that time was commercial artist, and it was thought of as someone who worked for a large corporation, a newspaper, magazine, or advertising agency. I never considered someone doing this kind of work for an individual. I just created the flyers and in reality was my own graphic designer.

There was no such thing as a personal computer like the one I'm using to write this book. I used a typewriter for my graphic design. I knew of three methods to finish them. I could go to the print shop and have them professionally reproduced. I could make copies with a Xerox machine. The third option was my favorite. I would make a Xeroxed flyer, leaving space for a picture. I would then take a picture, have it developed, have the picture reproduced fifteen or twenty times and then glue the copies of the picture to the flyer. I thought they were the best flyers ever, with a beautiful color picture.

Fun Fact

~ There's an Internet-enabled jacket which gives you a "hug" every time a Facebook friend likes your status.

Source: Dailymail.com

Now your agent uses their PC and designs all different types of designs that are much improved from the ones I created on a typewriter. Your agent's skill at graphic design will be utilized for advertisements, flyers, layouts of the properties, graphs, charts brochures, business cards, website designs, and more.

Email Communications

There was no such thing as email when I was a full-time real estate agent. Now it's part of the everyday job and is considered basic communication. There is an art to doing it right for you to have the most benefit. Email communications are easy, fast, and an efficient form of communication. It is a method one can confirm what was said and agreed to, or not agreed to.

Email is a fast and efficient method to send and receive much of the necessary paperwork and forms involved in real estate. Paperwork can be scanned and emailed or e-faxed to anywhere in the world. The receiver can then print, sign, scan, and email or e-fax it back. They can also use an electronic signature. The email communication is another art your agent has mastered to send and receive paperwork.

An email communication can be a tool to protect you from a costly lawsuit. Your agent, with the use of email, can document and communicate what is done, not done, said, not said, and what is disclosed, or not disclosed. An email can communicate exactly what is expected by all parties. An email can communicate the defects and potential defects concerning a property. A complete and organized email system is another layer of understanding, protection, and productivity that is provided for you by your real estate agent.

"Dreams about the future are always filled with gadgets."
~ Neil deGrasse Tyson

Email Marketing

E-mail marketing is the new mass mailings, an alternative or addition to the physical snail mail system that once was the only alternative to easily reach large numbers of customers. With email marketing your agent contacts buyers, sellers, and agents with a click. Like most things your agent does for you, it isn't exactly that simple. We talked about this subject in the Marketing Executive chapter. I'm also making the point here because email marketing is in the scope of information technology. Your real estate agent must know what they are doing to make their email marketing effective.

Here are some of the things that go into email marketing:

1. Any offer included
2. How often to share that information
3. How to follow up, and who to and how to respond
4. How to track the clicks and responses of potential clients
5. The data (names or lists)
6. What information to share
7. What links to include
8. What platform to use
9. What to do with the information you receive

Fun Fact

~ Sony researchers have developed a refrigerator that only opens when you smile.

~Source: University of Tokyo

Web Designer

Even when someone hires someone to do the web design they have to know what it is you want to accomplish with your website. I am in the process of building a website now and it has been an ongoing project. My designer can only build what I tell him to. He doesn't know exactly what it is that I want and need. We are, in effect, building it together. Your agent may do it her or himself, or in collaboration with a professional designer. No matter how it is designed your agent is involved. A well-constructed website can make your life easier. A well-constructed website will be an information resource for you, a kind of one-stop shop for you to have real estate information available for you.

Web Management

This may be one of the hardest jobs for your agent to keep their website up-to-date. A website isn't something you set up and then that's the end of it. It makes me laugh; it's kind of like when one gets married, that is just the beginning; you have to do something to keep it going. It is the same with a website. There is always something to take down, something to change, and something to add. This is just another of the tasks that may go unnoticed that your agent is doing for you.

Photographer

We spoke of your agent as a photographer in the producer chapter, and it also can be stated again here. Your agent is a true artist when it comes to photography. When you take pictures they must sell. They need to project an image of beauty and style. There is more to it than to point and click.

Conclusion

This is the electronic age and a real estate agent utilizes everything possible to assist you with your life and your real estate needs. Real estate is the cutting edge of the electronic era. In fact, there is a real estate franchise that was founded in 1972 called ERA. ERA stands for Electronic Realty Associates. This is proof that way back in 1972 that real estate was already thinking of moving in this direction. So much so there was a company that named itself after that. The founders of ERA Reality were amazingly insightful. I'll bet in 1972 they had no idea how right they were.

Technology is such a major part of all of life, and as the founders of ERA (Electronic Realty Associates) real estate knew back in 1972, it is even more applicable today. Your real estate agent is well-versed and proficient in the areas of information and design technology. This is all just another area that your agent is on the job for you.

"I have an almost religious zeal... not for technology per se, but for the Internet which is for me, the nervous system of mother Earth, which I see as a living creature, linking up."
~ Dan Millman

Recap - Information & Design Technology

Data Entry: submitting information into a database.

Database Manager: taking care of and keeping the data up-to-date.

Appraiser: estimating the value of real property based on factual analysis.

Graphic Designer: creating the layout for flyers, brochures, websites, emails and more.

Email Communications: using email as a form of communication.

Email Marketing: utilizing email to locate buyers and sellers.

Web Designer: your agent creates by themselves or with a professional to design a website that best serves your needs.

Web Management: taking care of all the adjustments and changes for the website.

Photographer taking pictures that sell and shine vs. pointing and clicking.

XVI. Data Analyst

"Alfred Hitchcock once told me, when I was analyzing a lot of things about his pictures, 'Clint, you must remember, it's only a movie."

~ Clint Eastwood
Actor, director, producer

The job and skill sets of your agent for life are vast. We are on chapter sixteen and there are still more tasks, skills, and jobs to discuss. Data Analyst is another aspect of the many tasks that your real estate agent performs on your behalf.

Unlike the Clint Eastwood quote, your home, and financial future is more important than a movie. The decision to buy or not to buy, sell or not to sell is one of the most important decisions of your life. Having an expert data analyst could come in handy in making buying and selling decisions. It just so happens your agent is an expert at analyzing data. In this chapter, you will discover how important analyzing data is to you and how your real estate agent provides that information for you.

"There's strong data that, within companies, the No. 1 reason for ethical violations is the pressure to meet expectations, sometimes unrealistic expectations."
~ Stephen Covey

Some of the data that your real estate agent analyzes are:

1. Agents
2. Buyers
3. Historical Data
4. Interest rates
5. Loans
6. Market trends
7. Market Values
8. Neighborhoods
9. Properties
10. Schools
11. Sellers

Your agent is an expert or close to an expert on nearly everything in this book and more. At this point you can get a real appreciation of all that your agent does for you. Being a Data Analyst is another of the many jobs, tasks, and skills that your agent utilizes on your behalf.

Inventory

Inventory is the real estate term for all of the homes for sale in a given area. The inventory is the most important data that your agent must analyze. He or she knows the properties that are for sale within their sales area. This is much more difficult than you might think. Consider that the data that your real estate agent is required to analyze is constantly changing. Properties go on and off the market every day. Prices are constantly adjusted, listings go expired, pending, sold, off the market, or canceled.

With all the fluctuation of hundreds of properties that must be analyzed, the inventory of properties for sale is yet another amazing feat that your agent performs for you that often goes unnoticed.

"Experts often possess more data than judgment."
~ Colin Powell

Market Trends

Your agent must not only keep up with the inventory, they must keep up with the market trends to best advise you. The biggest market trend is the prices in a given area. Are the prices going up or are they going down? Another trend is the pace of how quickly homes are selling. Your agent will know how many days the average listing in any given area is on the market before selling. Your agent will also keep track of the number of homes available at any given time. The number of homes on the market or the inventory is an important statistic for your agent to keep track.

Data

~ facts or information used usually to calculate, analyze, or plan something

Analyst

~ a person who studies or analyzes something

Source: Merriam-Webster

Buyers

Market trends aren't limited to property. Your agent is also aware of the trends of what buyers are doing. Are buyers more inclined to buy or are they cautious? Who are the likely buyers in an area? Are they younger, older? What is their typical income range? Do they tend to stay in their homes? Will they move in a few years? Do they have kids, and if so how many? When your agent has this data they are better equipped to find a buyer to buy your home and make your life easier.

Agents

Why would an agent be analyzing the data regarding other agents? By knowing who the other productive agents are, your agent can be more effective in selling your property.

When you are selling your agent is likely to know the top buyers or sales agents. Having a list of the top sales agents and using that list to market your property to those specific agents is a plus for selling your home. Your agent will also create relationships with these top agents. This is another advantage your agent for life will give you to get your home sold.

Knowing the top buyer's agents can be the difference between selling your property or not. In chapter twelve we talked about the 80/20 rule. The 80/20 rule states that 20% of the agents get 80% of the work done. Your agent knows who the 20% of buyer's agents out there who sell 80% of the homes. Your agent will market your home to these select buyer's agents to more effectively sell your properties. As an added bonus, these buyer's agents will be more knowledgeable and experienced and will be easier to work with, resulting in smoother escrows with fewer problems.

Sales and Sales Pending Properties

The sales and sales pending inventory are different than the, "for sale" inventory. Your agent must know the properties that have sold and the properties in escrow that haven't yet closed escrow. These are the primary properties your real estate agent will analyze to determine market value

Lenders

This is huge and extremely important for you as a seller and as a buyer. As a seller, your primary concern is to sell your property and get it in and then out of escrow. You have a desire to receive your proceeds and move on with your life. As a buyer, you want to get the lowest interest rate and payment. You want to qualify for the loan. Find the perfect home. Get your offer accepted and close escrow. The right and best lender is the most critical factor in achieving these goals. The art of funding a loan is a gift. Some people can pull a rabbit out of a hat and others don't know what I'm talking about. In fact, there could be a whole other book written called, *101 Reasons to Love Your Lender*. A lender can be your hero or your goat; you don't want the latter.

"It is a capital mistake to theorize before one has data."
~ Sherlock Holmes

The best method for your agent to analyze lenders is through experience, and by checking with other agents. To be clear I will discuss loans in a moment. Right now what I mean by a lender is not the company, but the person, the individual who will take the loan application and work the magic to get your loan funded and your escrow closed. Your agent will know which lenders to use and which lenders to shy away from.

Loans

The correct loan for the right buyer is key to having a property close escrow and close when they are scheduled to close. It is up to your agent to know a variety of loans from which to choose for a particular buyer. Yes, it is the lender's job to take care of the loan for your buyers. Your agent needs to be able to discuss the loans with their client to determine which programs are best for them and to answer a majority of their questions. Some loans are easier to qualify for than others. There are loans that are adjustable that would work best for a buyer who will only remain in a property for a short period of time. There are loans that have fixed periodic adjustments that work best for a buyer who's income will be stepping up to match the increases of the loan payment. Your real estate agent constantly analyzes the different types of loans to inform you of the different options available for you.

FUN FACT !

Fun Fact

~ It is estimated that Walmart collects more than 2.5 petabytes of data every hour from its customer transactions. A petabyte is one quadrillion bytes or the equivalent of about 20 million filing cabinets' worth of text.

Source: Harvard Business Review

Interest Rates

Along with lenders and loans, interest rates are also very important. Your agent will know whether the rates are headed up or down. They will assist you in determining when to lock in a rate. If the rates are headed up it is best to lock them in now. If the rates are likely to go down then it is better to wait. Your agent analyzes the trends of the market and interest rates and will advise you on his or her findings.

Economy

Your agent keeps tabs on the trends of the overall economy as well. The economy can help forecast the direction interest rates will be headed. The economy also helps determine prices and the trends for salary increases, all of which affect the real estate market.

> **"Personally I'm always ready to learn, although I do not always like being taught."**
> **~ Winston Churchill**

Neighborhood

You may have heard the expression neighborhood specialist. This term refers to an agent who does most of their work in a particular geographic area or neighborhood. They are familiar with the market trends, prices, styles, and models of properties, the schools, business, and people of that area.

Your agent may be a neighborhood specialist for a particular neighborhood, and they also have the ability to become an expert in any given neighborhood that they are working in. They accomplish this by doing research on the properties that have sold, are pending, never sold, and are currently on the market. They talk to other agents, lenders, and affiliates who are familiar with the neighborhood in question. They will even go door-to-door to learn about a particular neighborhood.

Conclusion

If you are getting the idea that your agent for life is truly amazing, **you are right**. The skill set of a data analyst is a major function of your real estate agent. Your agent has a vast variety of data to analyze and makes assessments every day to impact the quality of your real estate life, and ultimately your life.

The ability to take data and make sense of it is an art, an art that is only learned by experience, expertise, and a long-standing determination of excellence that your agent does for you. It also takes the determination to invest the time to daily analyze the data as it is continuously changing.

Recap - Data Analyst

Inventory: properties that are for sale in a given area.

Market Trends: the changes in sales, buyers, sellers, length of time on the market, and interest rates.

Buyers: people who are interested and are in the process of purchasing real estate.

Agents: one who is authorized to act for or represent buyers and sellers.

Sales and Sales Pending: property that has sold and closed escrow and properties that have sold and have not completed, or closed escrow.

Lenders: the individuals and their companies who handle the obtaining of the loan for the purchase of real estate.

Loans: a sum of money that one (a buyer) receives and promises to pay back including interest.

Interest Rates: the percentage of an amount of money that is paid for its use for a specified time.

Economy: the general outlook of the buying and selling of goods and services for a given area or country and in particular the sale of real estate.

Neighborhood: a group of homes in close proximity, it could be anywhere a from 3 to 300. It would usually have some sort of geographic identity separated by a large street, school, or business.

David Kline Lovett

XVII. Self-Promoter

"My main concern is meeting with the public because my main commitment, main interest is the promotion of human value, human affection, compassion, and religious harmony."

~ Dalai Lama
Buddhist Monk-Spiritual leader

The job of your agent is unique to many professions. Your agent, for the most part, has to promote themselves in order for you to find them. They also have to self-promote to find other buyers and sellers. They don't have to be P.T. Barnum, but they do demonstrate a myriad of methods to be discovered. This chapter goes into a few of the more traditional methods and some of the newer methods of self-promotion.

Client Referrals

Referrals are the lifeblood of the business for your agent. The highest and best compliment for any real estate agent is to receive a referral. For the average agent receiving a referral isn't easily accomplished; however, for your agent for life, it is a common occurrence. Why wouldn't you want your family and friends to have the best real estate experience and service possible? Referrals are the number-one method for your agent to be recognized and known.

Past clients or client referrals are a major and not the only source of your real estate agents referrals. A past client will know if an agent is honest, has integrity, is punctual, and honors their word. There is no better person to refer and advise you on the skills and ability of an agent than a past client.

ABCDE
FGHIJK
LMNOP
QRSTU
VWXYZ

Self-Promotor

~ the act or practice of promoting one's own interests, profile, etc.

Source: Merriam-Webster

Agent Referrals

An agent referral is a referral that comes from other agents. Your agent will earn these referrals by their body of work and the reputation they earn. This can be local agents, who for different reasons may want to refer their clients to the other agent. The reasons could be health, retirement, vacation, too much business, or they feel another agent is a better fit. Your real estate agent will also receive referrals from agents who are out of the area. Your agent can have a network of agents from all different cities and states who they can give and receive referrals from.

> "Without promotion, something terrible happens... nothing!"
> ~ P. T. Barnum

Doors

Yes, this is an old-fashioned method for your agent to be known, and yes, it still is effective. This means simply knocking on doors and asking people, "Who do you know who is considering buying or selling real estate?" That's all your agent has to do as far as knocking on doors.

It is important to note that your agent will door knock not only to be known but also for your benefit. If you are a seller they will knock doors around your home searching for people who are renters who may want to buy your property. They will also ask if a homeowner may know of someone who may want to purchase your property. This way they have an opportunity to choose their new neighbor. If you are a buyer they will be door knocking in areas of the properties that match the area, type, and price range you are looking for.

Associations

There are a plethora of associations that your agent can belong to. Your agent belongs to three real estate associations, their local association, state association, and the national association of realtors. Their local association of realtors is where they do the most networking.

Your agent could be a member of a local chamber of commerce, religious, trade, athletic, political, homeowners, educational, support group and many more associations where they can find referrals.

Fun Fact

~ The first known promotional products- commemorative buttons- trace back to 1789 when George Washington was elected president.

Source: Pomegranate Press

Friends and Family

I'll always remember Marty Rodriguez when she was an assistant to another agent, and then starting out as an agent on her own. Imagine, the future number-one C-21 agent in the world as a brand new agent. I recall, she had just raised her kids to a point where she felt she could work full-time and on her own. She had a large family, who along with her friends bought and sold property through her. The future number-one C-21 agent in the world was utilizing one of the basic methods to generate business and be well-known. Her family and friends. As the evidence of Marty becoming the number-one agent in the world, friends and family are a wonderful source to be known and to promote oneself.

Ads

As mentioned in the marketing executive chapter, your agent is an ad designer and writer. He or she uses ads to promote properties and also to promote themselves so you can find them and they can find you. They also make use of print, radio, Internet, television, email, YouTube, and social media to promote themselves.

"And let's be clear: It's not enough just to limit ads for foods that aren't healthy. It's also going to be critical to increase marketing for foods that are healthy."
~ Michelle Obama

Affiliates

It is possible that your agent can promote themselves with his or her affiliates, title representatives, escrow officers, termite inspectors, and home protection specialists who can assist them in finding clients, becoming known, and building a brand.

Conclusion

Your agent does it all, and self-promotion is another skill they have mastered. Even someone who is the best needs someone to be the best for. Self-promotion is necessary for you and your agent to be able to find each other.

Fun Fact

"The formulation of the problem is often more essential than its solution, which may be merely a matter of mathematical or experimental skill."
~ Albert Einstein

Recap - Self-Promoter

Client Referrals: obtaining clients from past clients, friends, and family.

Agent Referrals: referrals that originate from other agents.

Doors: your agent will canvas door-to-door to make him or herself known to you and to locate buyers and sellers.

Associations: real estate, homeowners, and trade associations are just a few more methods your agent uses to be known to you.

Friends & Family: your agent utilizes every possible source including family and friends to be of service to you.

Ads: all types of ads including email, website, print, TV, You Tube, radio, and more are utilized by your agent.

Affiliates: escrow, title, termite, home inspector, and home protection representatives are resources to produce buyers and sellers.

"That's a very convincing strategy."

XVIII. Project Manager

"Management is efficiency in climbing the ladder of success; leadership determines whether the ladder is leaning against the right wall."

~ Stephen R. Covey
Author & Educator

Your real estate agent's job includes that of being a project manager. When you are looking to buy or sell a property your agent manages the buying process. Your agent is also the project manager of the escrow. An escrow comprises the procedures involved in processing an agreement to its completion or closing.

The process of closing an escrow can be complex. The escrow process has the most problems and requires the most skill, tact, and know-how in a real estate transaction. Your agent will also be the project manager for many other tasks including the marketing of a property, locating financing, negotiations, and all projects that your agent provides for your benefit.

> **"I don't focus on what I'm up against. I focus on my goals and I try to ignore the rest."**
> **~ Venus Williams**

Loans and Loan Conditions

Loans and loan conditions are of major importance. Your agent often is required to monitor, look after, coach, coax, and motivate loan agents to get their job done and fund loans. Your agent is a pit bull for you to get your loans processed, approved, funded, and your escrows closed. A typical lender has multiple loans in process at a time. They may be lax in working with your loan. It is up to your agent to remind them and assist them in getting everything that is required (conditions) to fund your loans, and close your escrows.

Loan conditions are all of the items that a lender asks for and requires prior to the final approval and funding of a loan. Conditions can be any number of items such as bank statements, divorce settlements, pay stubs, and even medical records. A lender will ask for them to help satisfy themselves and their underwriter of the credit worthiness of a buyer. Your real estate agent will assist in getting the conditions satisfied. This can be the difference between a loan that never happens and the closing of a successful transaction.

> ## Project-Manager
>
> ~ the person in charge of the planning and execution of a particular project
>
> Source: Merriam-Webster

Paperwork

The very first purchase contract and receipt for deposit I saw back in 1984 was a single page. It was two pages by the time I wrote my first contract a few weeks later. And now the contracts are ten pages. Ten pages is just the amount of paperwork for the purchase agreement. There are counter offers, listing agreements, agency disclosures, lead-based paint disclosures, transfer disclosure statements, and many more. There are countless forms involved when a person signs their loan documents. Your agent must manage all of this and more.

Messengers

Messengers are as simple as Fed Ex, UPS, the U.S. Postal Service, and your agent her or himself. Some documents still must be original and often need to be taken from one place to another. Your real estate agent will make sure and manage any and all messengers required. Your agent, at a moment's notice, will pick up a document and make sure it goes wherever it needs to go.

Bill Paying

This is an example of something that could be a condition from the lender that is required to satisfy and approve a loan. Your agent will make sure that your bills get paid. This may sound like a simple task; however to some buyers and sellers it is a whole project on its own. When you stop to think about it, it can be a huge task that needs to be managed. Imagine you are a young couple just starting out in life. You and your spouse are trying to make it and looking to take part in the American dream by owning a home. Imagine you have a child in kindergarten, one on the way, a sick mother-in-law, a demanding boss, two car payments, and a mountain of student loans. Paying off one of the car payments in order to qualify for a loan can seem like a monumental task.

Yes, even the project of paying off a car loan isn't beyond the scope of your agent. I've done it many times where I set up a plan, brainstormed, and even arranged options for a buyer to pay off a loan or two. When you are the buyer and in the middle of a situation such as the one above, it isn't always easy to think of and execute on the project of paying off a loan.

Making Copies

Making copies sounds like I may be going too far here in explaining the tasks your real estate agent performs for you. Everybody at one time or another will make copies. Your real estate agent makes a lot more copies in doing their job than most others do in the course of their careers. Making copies may not fit as an individual project like managing an escrow, and it is a task your agent performs for you as part of their job.

Fun Fact

~ Myth – Project management
is pure paperwork.
In fact, a project manager
spends 90% of their time
communicating.

Source: Project Management Institute

Inputting Listings

Inputting listings makes me think of Louis. I loved Louis and the way she looked after and took care of me as a young and budding agent. Louis was in charge of inputting the listings of all 553 agents in the Glendora/Azusa Board of Realtors. Back then there wasn't the Internet and a computer system where we could do it ourselves. Now we can input the listing on our home computer, a tablet, or even a smart phone.

Inputting listings is an extremely important task that your agent performs. Unlike back in the time of Louis, listings and the information about a property for sale isn't just placed in the MLS (Multiple Listing Service). It is downloaded onto websites, social media, email marketing, print and electronic advertising. This is indeed a project of its own.

Writing in a way to best describe the properties is yet another major task. The art of presenting a property in the best light makes all the difference in whether a property sells and for what price. Your agent will make sure that your property is presented in its best light.

Listings

The handling of a listing or the marketing of your home is where your agent shines. It is where you will experience the benefits of working with a true professional. Managing and marketing a property or listing again could be the subject of another book.

Here is a partial list of the tasks that your agent manages in the handling of a listing:

1. Broker open houses
2. Checking permits with the city
3. Communications with buyers, agents, and affiliates
4. Determining an estimate of value
5. Locating the property to list/market
6. Major and minor repairs
7. Meeting agents, inspectors, contractors, repair, and maintenance people
8. Negotiating contracts
9. Open houses for the public
10. Pitching the listing at association and office meetings
11. Presenting the property for sale (MLS, social media, websites, email marketing, print and electronic advertising)
12. Problem solving
13. Promoting the listing to agents
14. Settling on an asking price
15. Showings
16. Staging of the property
17. Writing the description of the property

Escrows

If taking care of a listing is where your agent shines, the handling of an escrow is where they sparkle. Closing an escrow is where the pavement hits the road. It is where your agent shows his or her true colors. There cannot be too much praise placed on this element of your agent's job. If the escrow doesn't close, everything else is a waste of time. It's like getting all ready for the prom, buying the flowers, renting a tux, a limousine, making reservations at the best restaurant in town, getting a haircut, and a manicure and now your date doesn't show up. An agent can do all the work necessary to get an escrow to close and for a variety of reasons it may not. Closing escrows makes all the difference. It is either a 100% success or a 100% failure. Your agent will use all their skills, know-how, experience, determination, and even wit to close an escrow.

Your agent knows how to get the transaction closed. There are so many skills involved it's almost impossible to go over them all.

Here are some of the skills your agent utilizes to close your escrows:

1. Arbitrator
2. Coach
3. Connector of individuals
4. Contractor
5. Communicator
6. Counselor
7. Creative genius
8. Financier
9. Handyman
10. Jack of all trades
11. Lawyer
12. Magician
13. Negotiator
14. Politician
15. Problem solver
16. Project Manager
17. Psychologist

Ordering Inspections

Your agent's job as a project manager is one of making sure that inspections are ordered. In real estate, there is a plethora of inspections that must be completed by a variety of people. One inspection for every property where there is a loan involved is the ordering of an appraisal. It's not necessary to have an appraisal if a transaction is all cash. However, it is a good idea to ensure that the agreed-upon price is a fair price to all parties.

Your agent will also make sure that the termite inspection is completed. Your agent will make sure that everything that needs to be in the report is in order and that nothing is omitted. The same goes for ordering all the different inspections such as city inspectors, home protection, insurance inspectors, and more.

"Everyone has a plan: until they get punched in the face."
~ Mike Tyson

Planning

The job of your agent has a great deal of planning to it. Your agent can't afford to go out and just wing it. Your agent has a plan for everything. They plan their day, week, month, and year. To a large degree, they are planning your financial future. They have a plan for marketing your home. They have a plan for taking your home through the steps within an escrow to complete a successful closing. They have a plan to assist you after you have completed your sale. When you are looking to buy a property, your agent has a plan to find it, get it financed, and a plan to close the escrow.

You could say someone without a plan is someone without a clue. Your agent has a plan to guide you through every step of your real estate journey. Their plan could look much like a step-by-step checklist; their plan could also look like a mind map or a set of blueprints. The major point is that your agent for life isn't haphazard in assisting you and making sure that everything you need is taken care of.

"A good plan today is better than a perfect plan tomorrow."
~ George S. Patton

The Players

When you go to a sporting event you like to have a program so you are familiar with who the players are. In real estate, there are a plethora of individuals whom your agent must manage. This may sound strange, but the first person they must manage is you. You the buyer, seller, or in some cases both buyer and seller need to be informed and guided through the entire process. Again this is a subject that could have its own book written about it. One who has never been in a real estate transaction has no idea what is involved. With so much to be concerned about you can see why it is important to have someone who can assist or manage you along your real estate journey.

The second most important person to manage is the other agent involved in your transaction. Managing the other agent in a transaction is an art in and of itself. The problem is that agents are human beings and humans tend to not think or act rationally. Humans tend to want what they want, and not think of the larger picture. Typically a person doesn't consider what is fair and just for all concerned a priority. Humans tend to pick sides and want their side to win. An average person may be seeking to win so much that often they may overlook or fail to consider what is lawful or ethical.

The next and in many respects the most important person to manage is the loan representative or lender. The loan representative is the person who is responsible and has the power to make loans approvable, approved, and get them funded. Managing this person is imperative. Choosing the right loan representative is critical. I still have my favorite lender, Jill. There are several reasons why she is my favorite. Number one is that Jill gets the loans approved. Period. I don't always know how she does it, and frankly, there may be times I don't want to know. She has a tenacity that never quits. I've known her for almost twenty years as of this writing and she hasn't changed. She is a go-getter and simply gets it done. Make sure your agent has a lender like Jill. Having an agent who knows and works well with a lender like Jill is imperative.

We mentioned earlier that your agent manages your escrow. They also manage the person called the escrow officer. What worked well for me was to have a great relationship with them. The escrow officer is the quarterback for your transaction. They handle almost everything. Your escrow officer will make sure everyone and everything gets paid, funded, recorded, endorsed, notarized, signed, acknowledged, and taken care of. In short, a good escrow officer takes care of nearly everything. Your agent will have a personal relationship with their favorite one or two escrow officers. They will also have the ability to work well with an escrow officer who is chosen by another agent. Having a good relationship and the ability to work well with escrow officers is imperative and makes the difference between you having a smooth escrow or an escrow from you know where.

> **"Practice Golden-Rule 1 of Management in everything you do. Manage others the way you would like to be managed."**
> ~ Brian Tracy

Closing Date

Your agent will construct a structure for fulfilling your transactions and closing your escrows on the prescribed closing date. Closing an escrow on time may sound like an easy task. Trust me, it isn't. There are so many things that can alter a closing date that unless your transaction or escrows are handled by a professional they will most likely not close on the date the contract specifies.

The biggest obstacle to a translation closing on time is the loan. Lenders and loan underwriters are very cautious people. Their jobs depend on having as few loans go unpaid as possible. The best method for a lender to keep from having too many loans going back to the bank is to make sure they do their due diligence. The problem is lenders wait to the last few days before the closing date and then they ask for a boatload of conditions in order to approve the loan. In doing this they build a case for themselves if the loan goes bad. If the buyer is unable to satisfy the conditions they have a reason to disprove the loan.

Your agent sets up a structure to ensure transactions close and close on time. Here is the secret that saves you time, money, energy, and headaches. The secret is to work from the closing date backward. Your real estate agent's structure for completion starts with the closing date and works its way backward.

It will look something like this:

Closing Date	June 15th
Recording date	June 14th
Fund loan	June 13th
Submit loan for final approval	June 11th
Satisfy all loan conditions	June 10th
Receive final conditions list	June 7th
Satisfy initial conditions	June 5th
Receive initial conditions list	June 1st
Finalize loan package	May 28th
Finish processing checklist	May 25th
Complete all property inspections	May 12th
Oder all the inspections	May 8th
Begin processing loan	May 7th
Get all paperwork signed	May 6th
Open escrow	May 4th
Have all parties sign counter offers	May 3rd
Sign initial offer	May 1st

A structure for fulfillment is a proven system that will ensure that your loan gets approved and you close on time.

Conclusion

Your agent will take care of everything necessary to make your real estate transactions as easy for you as possible. The job of project manager makes sure everything and everyone is in order. Your agent will insure that everything happens when they are scheduled to occur with little or no drama.

Unless you read this book you wouldn't realize the complexity of the job of a real estate agent. Just the job of a project manager is a full-time job. There are many tasks and many players who carry out all the jobs involved in a real estate transaction who are managed by your real estate agent. Your agent is the conductor of a large orchestra with all the musicians and their instruments in perfect harmony.

Fun Fact

~ 95% of divorces are caused by a "lack of communication"

Source: Dr. Donald E. Wetmore

Recap - Project Manager

Loans and Loans Conditions: lending money with an agreement to repay. Conditions - requirements to finalize prior to a loan being approved.

Paperwork: a general term for all the forms that are required in a real estate transaction.

Messengers: someone who carries documents from one location to another.

Bill Paying: ensuring and doing the processes necessary to pay bills that are required to close a transaction.

Making Copies: another task executed by your agent.

Inputting Listings: submitting listing information into the MLS (Multiple Listing Service).

Listings: the entire process of offering for sale and the selling of property.

Escrows: handling a sale from the time when a buyer and seller make an agreement to the completion and closing of their transaction.

Ordering Inspections: the physical task of contacting and scheduling appointments for all inspections for a property.

Planning: a detailed outline for the achievement of the desired outcome.

The Players: all the people involved in a real estate transaction.

Closing Date: the day that a real estate transaction is scheduled to close or complete

David Kline Lovett

XIX. Communicator

"Wise men speak because they have something to say; fools because they have to say something."

~ Plato
Greek Philosopher

Your agent will communicate with you almost on a daily basis. There is a consistent flow of news that you will need to be informed of. It is also important for your agent to communicate when there isn't any news for a given day. An average agent is embarrassed and afraid to communicate if nothing has occurred. From an agent's point of view, it is not fun to admit and communicate that things aren't going according to plan. When things aren't going according to plan is exactly the time when you most need to know exactly what has or has not occurred. Your agent will do the hard thing and communicate with you, especially when there is no information to offer.

Be Clear

How does one get to Chicago, Illinois? The first step is to determine where you are. If you are trying to get from point A to point B, you have to be clear where point A is. It is the same with communication. You need to be clear and know what it is the other person is trying to convey. You will need to be especially clear if what the other person is trying to convey doesn't match your view of the facts or what you believe to be true.

Your agent will take the time and effort to discover exactly what is being talked about. What are all the facts and what is it the other person is really saying? Your agent will know the emotion being conveyed and their underlying and unspoken concern. Your agent will make sure and be clear about what is important to the person they are communicating with.

Communication

~ the act or process of using words, sounds, signs, or behaviors to express or exchange information or to express your ideas, thoughts, feelings, etc., to someone else

Source: Merriam-Webster

Egoless

The number-one quality of effective communications is to leave your ego at the door. This is precisely what your agent does. When one's ego is involved it is nearly impossible to communicate. What I have experienced for myself is that I, too, often find myself defending myself or my point of view. When I'm reacting and defending I'm not present to what is being said; in fact, I'm combative. You can see that this is no way to effectively communicate.

When you leave your ego at the door, you can hear what is being said. It is fascinating that when one stops defending, arguing, and interrupting before the other person's thought is fully expressed, how much understanding occurs. When you hear the entire thought or statement without the ego, the other person's idea isn't so confrontational. You can make sense of the statement from another point of view.

When your agent is confident with her or himself, when they can rely on their knowledge, expertise, and experience to allow them to check their ego, when they don't have to prove that they are knowledgeable, smart, or an expert, they can more easily bypass their ego for the sake of understanding.

I'll never forget a transaction that occurred in my office. Bennie was the listing agent and Cindy was the buyer's agent. They both were successful full-time agents and we all had worked together for a number of years and knew each other well. I noticed that Cindy and Bennie were having difficulties with their transaction. They had several heated arguments in the office. Both Bennie and Cindy fought for their client's point of view. I could see that neither one was listening to the other. They were so intent on winning that neither took a moment to hear what the other was saying. Cindy wanted the seller who Bennie represented to leave the flat screen TV with the home. Cindy argued that the way it was attached to the wall it was no longer personal property but a fixture. Real estate law says that a fixture is to be considered part of a property. Bennie argued that the TV was personal property and the sellers had every right to take it with them when they moved.

**"The single biggest problem in communication is the illusion that it has taken place."
~ George Bernard Shaw**

I could see both of their points of view. The seller had actually altered the living room wall so the TV was actually inside the wall. They had removed some of the drywall so the TV was flush or flat in relation to the wall. This was a legal issue. Is it personal property or a fixture? The problem from my point of view was that Bennie and Cindy didn't stop to ask their clients what they wanted. I had been watching and witnessing this argument for about two weeks when I stepped in and asked them, "Have you asked your clients what they want?" They both looked at me kind of stunned and at the exact same instant they both looked at me and said, "No."

I said, "May I suggest something?" and again in complete unison, they said, "Please." I said, "Why don't you both go to your clients and find out if the seller wants to take the TV with them and ask the buyer if they want the TV to stay." And then jokingly I said, "If neither one wants it, they could give it to me." Two days later when both Bennie and Cindy and myself were in the office together I asked them what their clients said. They both started laughing. The seller had a new condo that had no room for such a large television. The buyer was a scientist and never watched television and had a plan to have a painting specially made to fit in the space that the television was in.

Once their egos were left at the door, both Bennie and Cindy could see clearly and allow themselves the space to see what their client's needs were and not their own egos, the problem was solved. And the best part of it was that I got a new flat-screen television for free.

Positive Attitude

The Bible says, in Matthew 8:13 English Standard Version, "Let it be done for you as you have believed." If you believe you will have good communication, you will tend to have good communications. If you come into a conversation with the thought that this isn't going to be easy, this person isn't easy to get along with, or I just don't like him or her, you will tend to get exactly what you expect. When you have a positive attitude about who you are communicating with you will be better off. It is that simple to simply have a positive attitude and believe that all your communications will be positive, pleasant, and understood.

Compliment

One of the best ways to have good communication is to simply compliment the other person. Your agent knows that the best way to start communication is to compliment the person you are talking with. Giving even the smallest compliment will make the other person feel good about themselves. When you compliment someone they will be more likely to listen to your point of view. When they are willing to listen to you there will be improved communication.

We had just completed a property inspection on a property of a seller I was representing. The inspection revealed that despite the fact that the roof was only eight years old it was made with inferior materials and needed to be replaced. This was a $5,000 conversation. Rather than to just tell the seller, Bob, the bad news, I complimented him for the work he had done for the March of Dimes Foundation. This compliment made him feel better about himself. Bob could realize that he did contribute to humanity and he really did make a difference in the world. When Bob could see that the world was a better place because he was in it, he could be in a better place to hear that there was a problem with the roof. Communication was much improved, Bob understood the situation and we simply paid for the new roof from his proceeds from the sale.

Rapport

~ relation marked by harmony, conformity, accord, or affinity

Source: Merriam-Webster

Rapport

Your agent is a master at rapport. Having the ability to create harmony and accord in a relationship is essential for good communication. I had a situation where the buyers I was working with, John and Karen Lancaster, didn't fully understand the lending and approval process. They had been approved for a loan, and then they went out and bought a new car. The financing of the car altered their loan ratios and they no longer qualified for their loan. John and Karen were excited and eager to move into their new home. However, now they no longer qualified. What made things even more complicated was the fact that their current home was already sold and in escrow. John and Karen were facing the fact they might have to close escrow on the home they were living in and then not be able to move into their new home as they no longer qualified to buy it.

John and Karen were lucky enough to find a co-buyer with their aunt Suzi. The remaining problem was that they needed an additional three weeks to close the escrow. That meant that for it to work out for them, both escrows or transactions were going to need an additional three weeks to complete. Needing to extend two escrows an additional three weeks can be a deal breaker.

Fortunately, I created rapport with both the agent for the buyers of their old home and the seller of their new home. I connected with the buyer's agent because we both were involved in running, and the seller's agent actually knew my dad who was the town veterinarian. My dad had taken care of her pets for years. Thanks to the rapport I had gained through my relating to the other agents through running and my dad, John and Karen were given an additional three weeks to close the transactions and were able to move into their dream home without any additional complications.

Curiosity

You might think it's strange to say that it is an asset for your agent to be curious in communication. How do you think I was able to find out that in the above example that one agent liked to run and the other knew my dad? I was curious about their lives, I asked questions based on what they had said to me. Curiosity can be one of the best methods or ways of being to ensure there is good communication. Curiosity demonstrates you have a genuine interest in another person.

So often people assume they know why someone does or asked for something. This isn't necessarily true. Most of us are not mind readers. Just because someone asks for a Kleenex doesn't mean that they need to blow their nose. And for many of us, we assume that is what they want to use the Kleenex for. Without curiosity, there can not be complete communication.

What's What

The ability to know the dynamics of a situation is essential to handle a problem and to be effective in communication. It's like the concept of, how do you get from point A to point B? The first thing to know is exactly where you are. Once you know exactly where point A is, then and only then can you chart a path to point B. The ability to realize and determine the what's what of a situation is a skill that your agent has developed. In a real estate transaction, having the wisdom to

FUN FACT !

Fun Fact

~ People who have a strong friendship possess the ability to communicate with one another through facial expressions.

Source: funfacts.com

discover or uncover the what's what regarding a situation is a true characteristic of a professional.

Listening

It would seem that listening is an easy task and shouldn't be mentioned here. I understand the thought and need to explain there is listening and there's listening. We all have a voice in our head. It is the voice that talks to us constantly. It's the voice that analyzes, judges, and compares. Your inner voice is constantly talking and seems to never shut up. If it is constantly talking, constantly analyzing, judging, and comparing, how much listening are you doing?

The ability to quiet the voice in your head goes a long way in your ability to hear what is being said. For example, an agent could be explaining about a problem with the plumbing of a property and I might be thinking about their French accent and how cute it is, and then while she is explaining about the plumbing, I'm thinking about a vacation I took twelve years ago and how great the food was in Paris. This may sound silly but this inner dialogue goes on all the time and hinders communication.

"I like to listen. I have learned a great deal from listening carefully. Most people never listen."
~ Ernest Hemingway

Willing to Compromise

Your real estate agent doesn't have a win-at-all-costs attitude. Real estate is like life, there are problems, there are differing points of view, and there is always change. Without the willingness to compromise, one cannot be successful.

The willingness to compromise and leave one's ego at the door can be illustrated easily with the second most used document in real estate, the counter offer. If an agent insisted on their way and the original offer, very few agreements would be agreed upon. If an agent would only allow their seller to accept an offer that was full price there would be fewer sales. Property would stay on the market much longer and fewer buyers and sellers would get what they want.

A willingness to compromise is more than just negotiating a contract. Your agent has the ability to see and understand an issue from all sides. When you can see and understand things from all angles and have a willingness to compromise, magic happens, transactions close, and clients are happy.

Integrity

In order to have real communication, one has to have integrity. Webster's definition of integrity is, "the quality of being honest and fair and the state of being complete or whole." Integrity can be thought of being like a building or a bridge. The building or bridge has the integrity to hold a certain amount of weight in certain conditions. The integrity in this context is often stated on the side of the bridge on how much weight it is built to support. It is similar to your agent regarding integrity. Your agent has integrity in supporting you to get what you want.

Integrity can be demonstrated nearly every day in real estate. Your real estate agent will do what is expected but not stated or asked. This can show up as a follow-up call, a thank-you letter or showing up at a client's birthday party. Doing things that aren't promised but could be expected to do is one of the qualities that make your agent great.

Your real estate agent will also do what they know to do, going beyond what is expected for them to do. An example can be to not only send a thank-you gift to their client but giving a thank-you gift to the other agent. This is an example of what your agent knows to do and what was not expected. One wouldn't expect a gift from the other agent. Strictly from a business standpoint, you see that the agent who received the unexpected gift would be more inclined and excited to work in the future with an agent who has done what they know to do, even if it wasn't expected.

"The greatness of a man is not in how much wealth he acquires, but in his integrity and his ability to affect those around him positively."
~ Bob Marley

Another thing that your agent will do is complete work. They will not do things halfway or do just enough to complete a task. They will get things done in a complete fashion so that all parties are more than satisfied with what was done. Your agent will choose the better methods to complete a task and complete them in a timely manner.

Integrity is one of the most important aspects that your agent must have. Integrity includes being open and honest. It includes being fair to all parties and disclosing all material matters within a transaction. Integrity is also keeping and honoring one's word.

Feedback

There is no communication without feedback. In terms of a contract, there is no contract or agreement until the acceptance of the agreement is communicated back to both buyer and seller. For example, when a seller gives a counter offer to a buyer, the buyer accepting the counter offer doesn't complete the agreement. The agreement has to be acknowledged or communicated back to the seller that the counter offer was accepted to be a formally executed agreement.

The above scenario is a good example of feedback. With feedback, there is complete communication. If one can offer feedback to what was said then the person who gave the original communication will know what they are attempting to communicate has landed with the receiver and there is an understanding of what was said.

With feedback, the parties involved can adjust what they said in such a way as the other party can understand what they are saying. Feedback gives the person who spoke information regarding how well they were able to communicate what it was they were saying. Without the feedback, there is no knowledge that they were understood. Feedback allows for deeper communication and understanding.

Repeat

To repeat and enrollment covered in the next section are methods to improve communication. I learned about enrollment and repeating from a personal and professional development company called Landmark. In the context of this section to repeat means to reproduce or recreate what someone else has said. It means to repeat or paraphrase back to a person precisely what is it that they are seeking to communicate. When you repeat what someone says it can be an almost magical process. As you repeat what someone is saying you can understand and get an idea of the other person's experience. By repeating you will have a better idea of the mood, emotion, attitude, and state of mind of the person you are talking with. The person who is repeating knows more about the other person's mood and state of mind because they had to really listen to repeat what they said. To repeat or paraphrase what someone has just communicated builds rapport because the person whose statement was repeated feels heard.

A method to repeat what is being said is to listen to what is being said from a state of curiosity and wonder. A skilled listener is not guessing at what is being communicated. A skilled listener is not listening from a place where they believe or guess what is being said. Often, in the past, I would guess at what the other person was saying and where they were going with their communications. I wouldn't listen to them but think of what my response would be. I wasn't trying to be a poor communicator; it was what I automatically did. I believed I knew what they were saying.

Another aspect of listening is to get or understand the commitment behind what the other person is communicating, to understand what is shaping what is being said. In other words to listen for the commitment behind what is being spoken. By commitment, I mean the passion of the speaker.

Knowing what a person is committed to goes a long way in having effective communication.

Fun Fact

~ We listen to people at a rate of 125-250 words per minute, but think at 1,000-3,000 words per minute.

Source: Speakforsuccess.com

The last part of repeating is that it is almost magical when a person is repeated. You feel heard. You feel that your point of view has been recognized, acknowledged, and understood by the other person. No matter what one is saying it is a great feeling to have knowing that the other person really got what you were communicating.

Repeating helps make the other person feel heard. If you are complaining or arguing about something, much if not all of the impact of the problem you are complaining or arguing about disappears. When you are recreated the results of knowing you are heard are remarkable. Here is an example: The other day I called my sister to complain about a problem I was having with my love life and particularly with my girlfriend Emily. The problem was my girlfriend, Emily, wasn't my girlfriend, and I wanted her to be. The act of my sister repeating, "You are frustrated because you want Emily to be your girlfriend and she isn't." I felt heard, The magical part was that once Karen repeated my situation and my feelings of frustration behind it, THE FRUSTRATION DISAPPEARED.

Repeating is an important tool that your agent can use to create and maintain a real estate transaction. In real estate, there are problems almost daily. The art of repeating has the potential to make a real estate transaction much easier for all involved.

Here is an example of the power of repeating in real estate. Most problems that arise in a real estate transaction are when a loan doesn't get approved on time. When things don't go as planned, people naturally get upset. Often, we may be unnecessarily upset, angry, and unreasonable. These are the ingredients for a real-life problem that could be the beginning of the end of a real estate transaction. The end of a transaction means that a seller would have to put their property back on the market and start from scratch. For a buyer, it means that they, too, have to start at the beginning and begin looking at property all over again.

I had many transactions that had exactly this scenario. Most all buyers are buying the best and most expensive home they can afford. They are often right at the limit as far as qualifying. This was the case for James and Loretta. Their loan ratios were at the limit, and when their loan was submitted for approval there was about a 60% chance of the loan being approved. The particular underwriter on that particular day that James and Loretta's loan was submitted decided based on the information provided that the loan was a loan that should not be approved. The escrow transaction was in jeopardy and there was no way at this point that the agreed-upon closing date could be satisfied.

I called the listing agent Sherry. Sherry was furious. Her seller had a home to buy contingent on their current home selling. In other words, James and Loretta's loan had to close for Sherry's clients to move into their new home. I allowed Sherry to say everything she had to say about the matter. I mean everything. She went on for about five minutes. I took notes, and after she was done, the first thing

I did was to acknowledge her for who she was and her professionalism. Then I repeated what she had told me about the problems that had been created for her client as a result of the loan being denied.

Fun Facts

Studies by Fabio Sala at the Hay Group have shown that humor (used skillfully):

- Deflects critics
- Helps communicate difficult messages
- Improves morale
- Reduces hostility
- Relieves tension

Research by Bettinghaus and Cody (1994) and Foot (1997) showed that humor:

- Builds rapport and liking of the humorist
- Distracts the person from thinking about counter-arguments
- Makes the information more memorable
- Makes the person feel good and hence not think so carefully about the proposition
- Makes the target person want to listen more
- Relaxes the person, making them more receptive to the message

Obviously, this didn't disappear the fact that the loan was declined, but it did disappear Sherry's anger and frustration. Now we were at a place where we could talk about solutions. That is all it took. We extended the escrow by two and a half weeks. We introduced James and Loretta to Sherry's lender Bob, which made Sherry happy. Bob was able to get the loan approved in the allowed time. The repeating worked perfectly as everyone got what they wanted. All this because I learned the lesson of repeating.

Enrollment

Enrollment is what your agent does to motivate those who they are working with to be excited, interested, and moved. To enroll is to communicate an idea in such a way that the listener is excited and invested in that idea.

Enrollment for your agent is coming from a space of excitement and contribution to you and everyone around him or her. Your agent is out to make a difference for their clients.

Enrollment is:

- To be able to create agreements
- To be bold and brave enough to risk making mistakes
- To be committed to making a difference and contribute
- To be one who puts other's needs ahead of their own
- To be open to another person's point of view
- To be real and not try to just look good, or be there for your own purposes
- To be strong enough to allow others to fully express themselves
- To be the one who makes things happen…and close most any escrow
- To engage in conversation from a space of discovery
- To every day be dynamic and excited

- To listen and speak from a space of positivity
- To really listen
- To see people as potential for greatness

Enrollment creates a kind of agreement, which is uncommon in real estate. When another person is enrolling it's contagious. One almost can't help but be in agreement with a person who is enrolling.

"Any problem, big or small, within a family, always seems to start with bad communication. Someone isn't listening."
~ Emma Thompson

Fred was an old-time real estate agent, what one might call a good old boy. Fred was just happy. He didn't need a reason to be happy; he was always in a good mood. He wasn't happy because he was in a good mood; he was in a good mood because he was happy. Fred's good mood was contagious everywhere he went.

It was my third real estate deal I ever participated in. I was still nervous about most everything and didn't know what I was doing. I took Jake and Lucy to one of Fred's listings and they loved it. Everything was perfect except they were using an inheritance from their grandmother to finance the down payment, and it wasn't going to be available for five months. They thought for sure that a five-month-long wait for the down payment was a deal breaker.

Fred was so enrolled with life and everyone in it he seemed to be able to perform miracles. He met Jake and Lucy and fell in love with them. They were both just out of college, a brother and sister who were moving out from Michigan to start their lives. In their mid to late twenties, they had an innocence of being young, coupled with the wholesomeness of being from the Midwest. Fred took all that positive energy and was able to enroll the sellers to wait the five months to close escrow by sharing who Jake and Lucy were and by being his enrolling self.

Fun Facts

~ Having someone mirror your body language means they're interested in you and trying to build rapport.

Source: ArielSpeaks.com

Patience

The Charismatic Christian author and speaker Joyce Meyer wrote, "Patience is not simply the ability to wait-it's how we behave while we're waiting." This is exactly what great communication is about. Having the patience to allow the other person to fully express themselves without getting in the way, or more precisely allowing their ego to get in the way. Michelangelo shared that, "Genius is eternal patience." It can be the small things that make a huge difference, and one could look at patience as doing nothing. Nothing could make all the difference for you and your real estate transactions.

Your agent must have patience for you to decide to buy or sell. Your agent needs to have patience to wait for you to find the perfect home. Your agent is required to have patience when things don't go as planed, and things more often than not, don't go as planed. Your agent has the patience you need.

Respect

A simple attribute of your agent to be an effective communicator is respect. Respect is more than the idea that your agent is respectful of who he or she is working with. With respect, your agent will allow someone with an opposing viewpoint to fully express themselves. Having the respect and confidence to do this allows for communication of ideas, thoughts, arguments, and even frustration and anger. Allowing others to express their feelings is imperative to true communication. The ability to confidently respect another and their point of view is essential for true communication.

"Patience, persistence and perspiration make an unbeatable combination for success."
~ Napoleon Hill

Fun

Just about everything works better when it's fun, including communication. Your real estate agent uses humor and laughter to his or her and ultimately your advantage. When one can make light of what could be a potentially escalating situation, laughter and humor can calm tempers thus creating an environment where understanding, conversation, and communication can occur.

It still makes me laugh to think about 1435 Kanas Street. I was at the property with John and Sarah, the buyers whom I was representing along with the listing agent Tina Gonzales and the seller Mr. Jackson. We were at an impasse regarding the roof. John and Sarah wanted the seller, Mr. Jackson, to replace the roof. Mr. Jackson said that he had stipulated he was selling the property in, "as is" condition. John and Sarah contested that despite the sale being, "as is" the roof and condition of the property needed to be habitable. They said, "The roof's condition is at a point that it makes the property uninhabitable."

While everyone was in the living room arguing, I got on top of the roof to a spot above the living room where there was a hole large enough that I could see everyone and they could see my eyes looking at them. I started talking in my deepest Darth Vader voice and told them that, "The Lord was above them and the eyes of God were watching them." They all looked up very startled and confused, and then in my own voice I said, "I'm hungry. Whose turn is it to buy lunch?" They all started laughing and laughing. After I climbed back down from the roof, the listing agent and Mr. Jackson had already talked and agreed to replace the roof prior to closing the escrow.

The ability to put some light on the situation in a fun way was exactly what Mr. Jackson needed to see and hear for him to do the right thing and replace the roof. The humor was what made the difference.

"In order to carry a positive action we must develop here a positive vision."
~ Dalai Lama

Conclusion

One way your agent for life stands out from other real estate agents is in their ability to communicate. The ability to communicate is what prevents and solves problems. The ability to communicate is how people find their dream homes. The ability to communicate is what makes the difference between being able to sleep at night or toss and turn wondering if your home will ever close escrow. Your real estate agent is an expert when it comes to communication. Like a professional violinist or a top tennis player, your agent makes a difficult skill look easy.

Recap - Communicator

Be Clear: knowing exactly what is being communicated.

Egoless: letting go of the need to be right.

Positive Attitude: being upbeat with an intentionality for understanding.

Compliment: to tell someone that you appreciate them.

Rapport: having a mutual liking for another that is reciprocated.

Curiosity: displaying a sense of wonder and interest.

What's What: knowing exactly what the facts are in a situation.

Listening: hearing and understanding what is communicated with minimal interference from your inner voice.

Willing to Compromise: an ability to see the big picture and reach an agreement where everyone moves closer together.

Integrity: is a way of being whole, complete, honest, and fair.

Feedback: information that is communicated back to another with the intention of furthering understanding.

Repeat: the act of stating back to someone what they have communicated where they feel heard and satisfied.

Enrollment: having someone be excited, engaged, and interested in what you are saying.

Patience: in communication, it is the ability to allow another to fully express themselves without interruption.

Respect: the ability to honor another.

Fun: with humor and laughter there is improved understanding and communication.

XX. General Contractor

"The road to success is always under construction."

~ Arnold Palmer
Legendary golf professional

Aspects of your real estate agent's job are to act as a general contractor. He or she will often oversee, organize, and orchestrate, construction, fix-up, and work on real estate. The work could be anything from a remodel of a kitchen or bathroom, a new roof, to the planting of a flower garden. I took it for granted that jobs and tasks were completed on a property. When you are buying or selling your home it is often your real estate agent who takes on the job of general contractor.

Your agent looks after the details. He or she makes sure the plumbers, electricians, painters, landscapers, carpenters, inspectors, insurance adjusters, and engineers accomplish what they said that they would do. Your agent makes sure they do their jobs on time in a professional workmanlike manner. Few agents are actually general contractors; however, your real estate agent will often engage in the job of a general contractor. This chapter describes the activities your agent takes part in that are in the job description "general contractor."

Idea

As was stated in the introduction, things just don't happen by themselves. Everything begins with an idea, thought, or inspiration. There has to be an originating spark of inspiration that created the idea to make an improvement to a property. The idea often will originate from your agent. Imagine that a seller chooses to move to Houston, Texas and offers their home for sale and hires an agent to assist them. One of the major roles that agent will take on at the outset is to consider what will make the property more attractive for a buyer. The agent will brainstorm with the seller how to make the image of the home look sharp, enticing, and irresistible to a prospective buyer.

At this point, there is an idea, a thought, or an inspiration to put in a rose garden, a new garage door, or to paint the fence. Now that there is an idea, often it becomes the job of the agent to become a general contractor to transform the idea into reality.

FUN FACT !

Fun Facts

~ According to the California Contractors State License Board (CSLB), unlicensed contractors generate 97% of the 20,000 consumer complaints they get each year.

Planning

Once there is an idea then there must be a plan to execute the idea. Your agent is often included, and part of the overall plan that is laid out to transform the initial idea into reality. A plan can be as simple as to call a termite company to repair a damaged eave, to all the details involved in adding a second floor to a property. No matter what the plan is, your agent is often involved in making it a happen.

Contractor

~ a person or company that undertakes a contract to provide materials or labor to perform a service or do a job

Source: Merriam-Webster

Advising

Advising is an area where your real estate agent can really make a difference. Your agent knows what buyers are looking for. He or she knows what will be a difference maker in the value and desirability of a property. An agent can determine what needs to be done, what should be done, and what doesn't need to be done. When you are in the swirl of buying, selling, or both, you need someone who can show you and advise you on what to, and what not to do.

Collecting Bids

Your agent will often be the one to call a variety of professionals to gather bids for whatever job you are concerned about. Three or four bids for a job just don't appear at your door. Someone has to find the professionals to call, call them, meet with them, collect the bids, compare them, and assist in determining which one to go with.

Coordinating

Your agent is often the person who makes sure that everything regarding the job is taken care of. This includes the hiring of the company or person to do the work, meeting with them, and the coordination of the work. If the job requires more than one company or professional, the coordinating would be repeated with every single person and/or company involved. This includes but is not limited to inspections, estimates, work in process, final inspections, and job completion. Your agent is often the one taking care of everything.

"The only thing to do with good advice is to pass it on. It is never of any use to oneself."
~ Oscar Wilde

Paying Bills

The paying of bills is another task your agent performs for you. There was a technique that I often used when I was an agent acting as a general contractor when working with a seller. I submitted the payment of bills through escrow. This was a great way to make sure everyone would get paid and everyone was happy. Your agent can simply submit the bills into escrow, and when the escrow closes the bills are paid through escrow by the proceeds. This ensures that the funds are available and the professionals are paid.

Done Right

Water will take the most direct path pushed or pulled by gravity moving downward. Like water some tradesman and women who assist in making improvements on a property will do what requires the least amount of effort in completing work on a property. As a consequence, the work will not always be the best it could be. This natural way of being isn't necessarily in alignment with your desire for your property to have high-quality workmanship.

"He that is good for making excuses is seldom good for anything else."
~ Benjamin Franklin

Your agent will ensure that the quality of work is up to standard and that, "you are getting your money's worth." Quality workmanship in repairing or replacing a garage door can make the difference between a sale occurring or not. I love what Henry Ford had to say on quality, "Quality means doing it right when no one is looking." Your agent will help ensure that the work will be completed on time and done right.

For most every property there will be a job done to either get the home ready for sale or to be in compliance to a buyer or lender's request prior to closing. The job could be anything from repairing a leaky roof to a broken window.

There was a seller named Mrs. Arnold. The home inspection revealed a small yet consistent leak under the kitchen sink. Mrs. Arnold desired to be in compliance and gave the responsibility for the job to her grandson Jimmy. Jimmy was a good guy who was between jobs. The work on the house was a way Mrs. Arnold was helping Jimmy make some money until he found employment. She had Jimmy paint and clean all around the home to get it ready for sale. The last item was to repair the leak to close escrow. Jimmy was trained as a sales representative for an automotive fuel additive company and had been laid off. He was not a plumber nor a handyman. Mrs. Arnold didn't realize how much trouble Jimmy was having under her kitchen sink.

Mrs. Arnold's agent did something that I will never forget. Ginger recognized that Jimmy was not getting the sink repaired in the manner that would satisfy the buyer. She had a conversation with him about the automotive fuel additive industry and enrolled him into looking for a job. Jimmy had so much enthusiasm after the conversation that he informed his grandmother that he could no longer work on the sink. This allowed Ginger to move her best handyman Larry to take care of the sink.

Everyone was happy, no feelings were hurt, and most importantly, there was no delay in the closing of the property due to the sink not being repaired up to standard. There were no phone calls after closing by an unhappy buyer. Ginger was truly a great agent for Mrs. Arnold and the buyer who, like the Henry Ford quote, "Quality means doing it right when no one is looking" didn't even know about the problem.

Putting out Fires

Putting out fires is where your agent shines. What I mean by fires are problems. In real estate, there are all kinds of problems, and for many of them they will seem to anyone but your agent to be unsolvable. To your real estate agent, the unsolvable problem is just another day at the office. There are several qualities that stand out that make your real estate agent for life special in the area of putting out fires:

1. A getting it done-NOW mentality
2. Calmness
3. Connections
4. Communication
5. Critical thinking skills
6. Egoless
7. Positive attitude
8. Teamwork
9. The ability to not overreact

As you can see from the list your agent has a plethora of qualities, gifts, and talents. There are many things that can and will go amiss in a real estate transaction that gives your agent an opportunity to shine.

Managing

A general contractor is like a conductor of an orchestra. They make sure everyone does what they have agreed to do in the time they have agreed to do them. A general contractor helps the owner determine what projects they will do and not do. They also help an owner decide and choose how to complete the projects. Your agent will advise an owner which tradesmen to use, what is to be upgraded, and how to do it. Managing is overseeing, advising, and making sure things are finished in a workmanlike manner.

How many times have you had some work done and it wasn't done to satisfaction? The main reason this happens is because there isn't proper management during the work process. It is good to know that there is another set of eyes overlooking your project. You will have the satisfaction of knowing that there is someone who knows what needs to be done and how it should be done. Remember, your agent has experience managing work on projects. He or she knows what to look for, what to expect, and how to get the job done in an excellent, professional, timely manner.

"No problem can be solved from the same level of consciousness that created it."
~ Albert Einstein

Conclusion

The job of a general contractor is nowhere to be found in the training manual to become a real estate agent or on the real estate examination. Performing the duties of a general contractor is just another of the many jobs, tasks, and services that are included in the job description real estate agent. Your agent does much more for you than expected.

Recap - General Contractor

Idea: the genesis of something new.

Planning: a set of steps to transform an idea into reality.

Advising: input, thoughts, and options for completing an idea.

Collecting Bids: the activity of obtaining options to complete a job.

Coordinating: putting people, places, and things together.

Paying Bills: the process and steps of reimbursement.

Done Right: to efficiently accomplish and complete a job.

Putting Our Fires: dealing effectively with problems.

Managing: coordinating and controlling the process of work.

XXI. How to Find Your Agent

"The best way to find yourself is to lose yourself in the service of others."

~ Mahatma Gandhi
Leader of India

Here we are at the end of this book. It is my intention that by now there is absolutely no doubt in your mind that the job of your real estate agent is a huge task. You know what qualities to expect, look for, and to never settle for anything less than. You will now insist on having an agent who will assist you with your real estate needs and beyond. And lastly that you can now more fully appreciate the size and scope of the job of a real estate agent. This chapter will give you the methods to find your real estate agent for life. The agent you are looking for will put others' needs ahead of their own. If the process of finding your agent takes some time and effort, remember that you only have to do it once.

Referral

Your real estate agent uses referrals to find clients, so why not use the same method to find your agent? Ask-Ask-Ask. You ask your friends and family for a referral or their opinion when looking to buy a new car or choosing what movie to attend. Talk to your friends, family, co-workers, neighbors, classmates, and everyone you interact with. Just ask, "Do you know of any amazing real estate agents?" Have them give you at least two or three stories about what they have done to earn their trust and respect. Have them share what type of person they are. How do they treat their own family? Are they punctual? Do they do what they said they would do when they said they would do it?

"Friendship is born at that moment when one person says to another, What! You too? I thought I was the only one."
~ C. S. Lewis

After finding a potential agent for life, get a second or third opinion to insure he or she is the right agent for you. Ask your potential agent for life for the names of prior and current clients. Make sure to ask for and get more than one reference. You get a second opinion when going to the doctor. You get multiple quotes when you are painting your home. You call more than one prior landlord when vetting a prospective tenant. Do the same when vetting perhaps the most important professional you will ever work with.

Brokers

You can call a broker and/or owner of a real estate company to locate an agent. Simply call an office and ask to speak to the manager, broker, or owner and explain to them you are looking for an agent to work with, an agent for life. Explain to them you want an agent who has the qualities and attributes listed in this book. Better yet, give them a copy of this book. If they give you a name or two, ask them about the agent's work ethic, integrity, and impeccability.

You will then have to interview that person to determine if they are someone whom you will want to work with. We will go further into the interview process at the end of this chapter.

Broker

~ one who is licensed by the state to carry on the business of dealing in real estate

Source: The Real Estate Dictionary

Friends & Family

One of the greatest and often most untapped sources for information is your friends and family. I believe for most of us we tend to assume that our friends and family don't have the information or answers to the questions that we are looking for. I think I know all about their lives and what they have been up to. The truth is I have no idea who they know or all the people that they have connections and contacts with.

The key is to simply ask, "Who do you know who is an outstanding real estate agent? Do you know of anyone who has gone far and away beyond what is expected in service of others in the field of real estate?" Then be quiet and listen to what they say. I know I was amazed to hear that so many of my friends and family actually knew or they knew of someone who has worked with a real estate agent who was outstanding.

Another link that we wouldn't necessarily be thinking of would be that the agent who our friends or family may have known may know of another agent who they can refer who is amazing. A method you can use is to state you are looking for a specific agent who performs the services in this book. They will be more likely to refer you and less likely to steer you to themselves when they hear all the qualities, services, and skills that you are seeking in your real estate agent.

"Choosing to be positive and having a grateful attitude is going to determine how you're going to live your life."
~ Joel Osteen

Expect

I fully believe that we get what we expect out of life. Jesus said, "It is done to you as you believe." The Buddha stated, "You become what you think about." If you expect to be, do, or have something, expect to have it and whatever it is will tend to happen. Expect and know that your perfect agent has already found you. Know that the perfect real estate agent is already on the way to be of service to you.

To expect or know that you already have found your agent is like a prayer. When one prays one is essentially saying to God that you are in agreement with the fulfillment of your prayer. It is a spiritual law that you tend to get what you expect. Expect and believe that you already have your agent for life.

Signs

You can get an idea of what agents are popular and successful by the signs that you see in an area. To be clear, the agent who has the most signs in an area doesn't mean that they are the agent for you. All it means is that they have the most signs that you saw in an area. They are at the very least active in the area. A real estate sign is a great place to start your search because:

1. It has a phone number attached that you can call.
2. It is attached to an agent who has some degree of success.
3. It is in the area you are looking to buy or sell.
4. You can call to gather information about the area, home, market, and market trends.
5. You'll get an immediate idea of the agent by how your call is handled.

Google

Is there a better source than to Google a subject? To be fair you can utilize any number of search engines. Bing, Yahoo, Ask, and AOL, are just a few that are not named Google. The point is that you can look from your computer, laptop, tablet, or smart phone for your agent. You can utilize Google to find an agent and to learn about them. Try this out for yourself. Search your own name. Search and discover about yourself as if you are learning about an agent to discover if they are the agent you want to work with for life. You will be

"Being deeply loved by someone gives you strength, while loving someone deeply gives you courage"
~ Lao Tzu

surprised at how much information that is available. You will find much more than you may have thought would be there. You may find more than you would like to see. You may find that you should have been more careful what you posted on social media.

With an Internet search, you can act like a detective to determine if an agent you have met truly is the agent you want to work with. You will then need to do your due diligence to determine whether or not they are the one. Some of the qualities to look for when searching their name are listed at the end of this chapter.

Website

Most every agent will have a website. You can use a website to help determine if an agent is one you want to work with. A great website doesn't ensure a great agent; it is just an indication. If there is no website or it is out-of-date, dysfunctional, or inaccessible, you can be almost certain that agent is not the one. A website is also a place that you can locate testimonials that you can read and then verify to assist you in your search.

Testimonials

A written or a video testimonial is just a beginning. It's great that a prospective agent has a few testimonials on their website or at hand to share with you. Having a few shows that they have been in the business and (if they are real testimonials) they have worked with these individuals and they were pleased with their performance.

Fun Facts

~ It is a legal requirement in New York for a property seller to disclose if the property a client is inspecting is believed to be haunted by ghosts.

Source: crazyfacts.com

Read or watch them all. Learn what others have said about this person. Listen for the qualities that you are looking for. Don't be fooled by a bunch of hyperbole. You want to hear real, definable actions that the agent performed. For example, don't settle for a description like he or she did amazing work. What was it that was amazing? Look for a story of an agent going the extra mile. Picking your son up from school. Driving a set of documents from one location to another when the courier didn't show up. Personally paying the painter or carpenter for the work needed to satisfy a lender to get a deal closed.

Take it a step further. Call the people who gave the testimonials. Google them. Call them like you are a rental manager and you are researching a prospective tenant. Call to verify that the testimonials are real. Ask them if they know the person. Don't offer that they are a real estate agent. Just offer the person's name. Do they know immediately who you are talking about? Ask them about their relationship and about the testimonial. If it is something they made up, chances are they won't remember. If it was truly an incident where it changed their life they will remember. If the stories don't match up, run. Go on to the next agent and repeat the process.

Know that there is more to the screening process than simply having a valid testimonial. It is imperative to have the testimonial be valid. However, it isn't the only criteria. Again, make sure you go through the list at the end of this chapter to ensure you find your true agent.

> "Be slow in choosing a friend, slower in changing."
> ~ Benjamin Franklin

Text Test

What I mean by test text is to call, text, and email your prospective agent and note the response and response time. Yes, it is possible a great agent may not respond because of an emergency. For the most part, how a person responds the first time is an indication how they will respond every time. Send a text, make a phone call, and deliver an email. Did they respond quickly, professionally, and were they diligent in getting your questions answered? Were they polite, courteous, and articulate with their response?

Take Your Time

One of my biggest problems is that I'm often in a hurry. I have been one of those people who wants things immediately. When I go shopping for clothing I want to buy something. To me shopping is a waste of time; buying is productive; anything else doesn't even make sense. The last thing I want to do is take my time. When you are looking for the person who is in charge of your largest investment of your life, it is imperative that you take your time.

You may be in a hurry to get started and find your dream home or sell a property you have owned for a while. You have plans, goals, and dreams you want to complete. It's like choosing your husband or wife. How many people married the first person who seemed like they might be the right one and got divorced less than a year later? It is no different when choosing your agent for life. Take your time and make sure you have the right one before you move forward. You will be glad you did.

Don't Compromise

You deserve the best. Just like the last point, take your time. You should never compromise. Don't settle for less. You should never have to suffer dealing with mediocrity. You deserve:

1. to have an agent who knows what they are talking about.
2. to have an agent who will get the job done.
3. to have an agent who will respond to you in a timely fashion.
4. to have an agent who will think of you before themselves.

Don't settle for anything less in your agent. You should never compromise.

You Will Know

You know when something is right. When you meet your agent you will know it. It's a bit like meeting that special someone, that person who sweeps you off your feet and you can't think about anything but them. Your perfect agent will feel like a long-lost friend or your favorite aunt or uncle. Your agent will have a reverential quality of competence, connection, assurance, and intellect. Your agent will make you feel like the world is as comfortable as your own living room. You will be sure you have the right person in charge of your real estate needs.

Interview

You will want to have an interview with any and all potential agents.

Below, is a pre-interview checklist:

1. Call at least two of their testimonials to verify their authenticity.
2. Has the prospective agent passed the text test?
3. Have they passed your Google search?
4. Locate a potential agent.
5. Review their testimonials.
6. View their website. Did they pass your criteria?

Only after a prospective agent has passed the items on the checklist do you set up an appointment for an interview.

> **"Love can only be found through the act of loving."**
> **~ Paulo Coelho**

The interview is important and so often left out. Like a relationship, we often stay with the one who is ready and available and hope that it will work out. We don't take the time necessary to make sure we are in a relationship that will be most beneficial to all parties. We don't want to invest the time or feel it's too much work. It might be insulting to the other person if we check out their credentials. If you want a life that matters, a life that works, you have to do the work.

The fact that you insisted to take the time to sit down with an agent will set you apart from 95% of their clients. You will earn respect by insisting on an appointment, which will translate into better service.

An advantage of insisting on having an interview is that it will be a barometer to test your prospective agent. Listen and pay attention to how they react to your request. Do they hesitate? Do they question? Do they ask you why? If they question, what are their questions? Are they trying to get out of the interview, or do they welcome it?

Questionnaire

Once you have an interview you need to know what questions you want to ask, and more importantly, you must have a clear intention for the meeting. Your entire quest, goal, motive is - are you my agent for life? That is it. You must not compromise. This is your life and just because an agent has three kids and one who is sick doesn't mean that they are the best agent for you. They will be taken care of by a power higher than you. You don't have to be the one to save them.

This interview is very simple. The interview has one objective; is the person I'm interviewing the agent for me? Here are some things to look out for and some thoughts to get you started.

1. Did he or she ask you questions to clarify your motivations?
2. Did he or she build rapport?
3. Did he or she listen to you?
4. Did he or she look you in the eye?
5. Did they provide a list of references?
6. Did they provide a professional resume?
7. Did they take over the interview or give you space to talk?

8. If you can, look at his or her car. Is it clean and organized?
9. Was he or she dressed professionally and well-groomed?
10. Was he or she likable?
11. Was he or she on time?
12. Was he or she respectful?
13. Was he or she willing, excited, and prepared for the interview?
14. What did he or she do when you started the meeting?

First impressions go a long way in forging personal and professional relationships. Chances are you will know within the first six seconds if this is a person whom you want to continue having an interview with. I suggest having a plan in case you know early on this isn't the right person so you can shorten the interview. It does no one any good to go on for an hour when you know they are not someone you will be working with. Don't make up an excuse or have someone set up to call you like they are saving you from an unpleasant date. Just be honest, thank them for their time, and let them know you are interviewing other agents and you will get back to them. They don't know how many questions you had prepared to ask.

If you do choose to go on with a full interview, here are some questions you can ask:

1. How is your relationship with your family, mother, and father?
2. How long have you been in real estate?
3. If you could do anything with your life, what would it be?
4. If you had to change to another profession, what would it be and why?
5. Tell me about your favorite and least favorite clients.
6. Tell me-why are you in real estate?

7. What are the three most important lessons you have learned working with clients?
8. What are your top five values, and why?
9. What does the word integrity mean to you?
10. What do you like most about your job?
11. What do you like the least?
12. What has been your most gratifying moment in real estate?
13. What makes you mad, and what makes you happy?
14. What would you like to see less of in real estate?
15. What would you like to see more of in real estate?

These questions are just a baseline. You can use them all, cut a few, and add a few of your own. The point is to determine if the person in front of you is your agent for life.

> **"We must let go of the life we have planned, so as to accept the one that is waiting for us."**
> **~ Joseph Campbell**

Conclusion

I can't help but think of the phrase, "When the student is ready the teacher will appear." It could be that when you are ready your agent will become available to you. He or she could be someone you already know. Your agent may be someone you know from church, your dance class, or even high school. It is true when you put in the effort to seek, you shall find. In Luke 11:9 (NIV-New International Version) it states,"So I say to you: Ask and it will be given to you; seek and you will find; knock and the door will be opened to you." Can it really be this easy? The answer is, yes it can.

The point made above is that you have to be active in finding your agent. You have to do something; you have to take action. There is a Quaker saying, "Pray and move your feet." Yes, prayer can be another method or tool, but unless you do something, getting the results you desire is unlikely.

The other sections of this chapter give you some things that you can do in order to get your feet moving in the direction of finding your agent. Any one of them will assist you in locating your agent. What matters is that you find the best possible real estate agent.

Once you find a prospective agent, it is just as important to vet them, to make sure that they have the qualities that you are looking for to be your real estate agent for life. See the list in the appendix section to get an idea of some of the qualities that your agent must provide.

Recap - How to Find Your Agent

Referral: a recommendation.

Brokers: people who are licensed by
                                 the state to carry on the
                                 business of real estate.

Friends & Family: people who may be a
                                 resource for you to locate
                                 your agent.

Expect: a knowing and anticipation of
                                 a desired outcome.

Signs: real estate for sale signs.

Google: use the Internet for your
                                 search and vetting.

Testimonials: statements explaining the
                                 qualities, abilities, and
                                 diligence of an agent.

Text Test: a test to determine how quickly and responsibly an agent communicates.

Take Your Time: a warning not to act too quickly when choosing an agent.

Don't Compromise: only work with an agent who is a great agent.

You Will Know: an inner intuition when something or someone is right.

Interview: sitting down with a prospective agent in order to determine if they are your real estate agent for life.

Questionnaire: a list of questions to ask an agent at the interview.

XXII. Final Thoughts

"We are what we think. All that we are arises with our thoughts. With our thoughts, we make the world. "

~ Gautama Buddha
Founder of Buddhism

I first want to say it was a pleasure and honor to write this book. This book is dedicated to all the hardworking real estate agents in the world. It is too often in this world that we humans don't appreciate and acknowledge each other. After working as an agent and broker since 1984, I realized there were many varied tasks involved in the job of being a real estate agent. Until I wrote this book, I had no idea how vast, complex, and varied the job of being a real estate agent really was. Much of the time an agent is not only unappreciated but put down for seemingly doing almost nothing and receiving large commissions. This book was written to counter that thought and bring light to the art of being a real estate agent.

This book was written with three objectives in mind:

1. For you to be able to know the distinction between an average real estate agent and a great agent.
2. So you the reader can understand and appreciate the size and scope of a real estate agent's job.
3. To assist you in identifying and finding your agent for life.

It is not until one fully looks at something do we know what that subject or activity is all about. The art of real estate is varied and complex. I didn't fully comprehend the scope of the job until I wrote this book.

As I mentioned in the acknowledgment at the beginning of this book, I appreciate all the clients, teachers, agents and brokers I worked for and with over the years. Without them, I wouldn't have the experiences that allowed me to understand this amazing profession known as a real estate agent. I would never have grown and come to know what it is to be a great agent. I would never have known what it is to serve and assist clients in what may be their largest investment and the most cherished endeavor of owning a home.

It is my wish that you the reader, client, homeowner, and future homeowner can comprehend the size, scope, hard work, and expertise that goes into this profession. For you to fully appreciate all that is done on your behalf and for you to be able to find your real estate agent for life. I wish you the best.

David KLINE LOVETT

Appendix 1

Qualities to look for in an Agent:

1. Compassion
2. Communication skills
3. Compassionate listener
4. Experience
5. Expertise
6. Honesty
7. Hygiene
8. Impeccability
9. Integrity
10. Knowledge
11. Likability
12. Loyalty
13. Neatness
14. Organization
15. Poise
16. Professionalism
17. Rapport skills
18. Responsibility
19. Selflessness
20. Sense of humor
21. Style
22. Timeliness

Appendix 2

Interview Questions:

1. How is your relationship with your family, mother, and father?

2. How long have you been in real estate?

3. If you could do anything with your life, what would it be?

4. If you had to change to another profession, what would it be and why?

5. Tell me about your favorite and least favorite clients.

6. Tell me-why are you in real estate?

7. What has been your most gratifying moment in real estate?

8. What are the three most important lessons you have learned working with clients?

9. What are your top five values, and why?

10. What does the word integrity mean to you?

11. What do you like most about your job?

12. What do you like the least?

13. What makes you mad, and what makes you happy?

14. What would you like to see less of in real estate?

15. What would you like to see more of in real estate?

Appendix 3

Things to notice when interviewing a prospective Agent:

1. Did he or she ask you questions to clarify your motivations?
2. Did he or she build rapport?
3. Did he or she listen to you?
4. Did he or she look you in the eye?
5. Did they provide a list of references?
6. Did they provide a professional resume?
7. Did they take over the interview or give you space to talk?
8. If you can, look at his or her car. Is it clean and organized?
9. Was he or she dressed professionally and well-groomed?
10. Was he or she likable?
11. Was he or she on time?
12. Was he or she respectful?
13. Was he or she willing, excited, and prepared for the interview?
14. What did he or she do when you started the meeting?

Appendix 4

101 Reasons

To Love Your Real Estate Agent

Your Agent is your:

1. Accountability Partner
2. Ad Designer
3. Ad Distribution Expert
4. Advisor
5. Ad Writer
6. Appraiser
7. Arbitrator
8. Assistant Escrow Coordinator
9. Bill Payer
10. Bolger
11. Cheerleader
12. Closer
13. Coach
14. Concept Designer
15. Connector
16. Coordinator
17. Comedian
18. Communication Expert
19. Compassionate Listener
20. Confidant
21. Contractor
22. Counselor
23. Creative Genius
24. Data Analyst
25. Data Base Manager
26. Data Entry Technician
27. Deal Maker
28. Design Technologist
29. Detective
30. Document Signing Specialist
31. Dream Maker
32. Director
33. Driver
34. Email Communications Expert
35. Email Marketer
36. Escrow Closer
37. Escrow Supervisor
38. Financial Consultant
39. Fortune Teller
40. Friend
41. General Contractor
42. Graphic Designer
43. Guru
44. Handyman/woman
45. Home Finder
46. Information Technologist
47. Insulator Against Liability
48. Interior Designer
49. Internet Marketer
50. Inventor
51. Jack of All Trades
52. Law Consultant
53. Lighting Technician
54. Lingo Translator
55. Listing Supervisor
56. Loan Manager
57. Lobbyist
58. Organizer
59. Magician
60. Manager

61. Marketing Executive
62. Motivator
63. Messenger
64. Money Maker
65. Negotiator
66. Partner
67. Peace Maker
68. Photographer
69. Physical Mail Facilitator
70. Planner
71. Politician
72. Printer/Copy Maker
73. Presentation Expert
74. Production Designer
75. Production/Engineer/ Mastering/Editor
76. Producer
77. Problem Solver
78. Project Manager
79. Prayer Partner
80. Psychologist
81. Radio Advertiser
82. Real Estate Consultant
83. Real Estate Resource
84. Referral Provider
85. Salesman
86. Self-Promoter
87. Spiritual Advisor
88. Social Media Expert
89. Supporter
90. Stager
91. Teacher
92. Teammate
93. Termite Advisor
94. Television Advertiser
95. Time Manager
96. Troubleshooter
97. Videographer
98. Web Designer
99. Web Master
100. Writer
101. YouTube Star

Appendix 5

Questions you should ask to determine an agent's experience:

1. How can I best help you help me? (Yes, just like Tom Cruise said in *Jerry Maguire*.)

2. How long have you worked full-time in real estate?

3. How many transactions have you closed?

4. What have you found to be the biggest problems?

5. What have you found to be the most successful formula for success?

6. What mistake have you learned the most from making?

7. What skills have you gained and improved upon since becoming a real estate agent?

8. What were your solutions to your bigger problems?

Appendix 6

Professionals Your Agent Works With:

1. Appraisers
2. Carpet and floor installers
3. City Inspectors
4. Contractors
5. Credit repair specialists
6. Electricians
7. Escrow officers
8. Handymen
9. Home protection insurance agents
10. Inspection companies
11. Landscapers
12. Lawyers
13. Lenders/Banks
14. Loan processors
15. Painters
16. Plumbers
17. Property insurance agents
18. Roofers
19. Termite inspectors
20. Title representatives

Appendix 7

Areas Where Your Agent Negotiates for You:

1. Clean-up

2. Closing dates

3. Commissions

4. Considerations

5. Contracts

6. Escrow

7. Fixtures

8. Interest rates

9. Move-in dates

10. Movers

11. Personal property

12. Price

13. Rental agreements

14. Rent back

15. Repairs

16. Termite

17. Terms

Appendix 8

Other Areas Where an Agent Can Help You:

1. Creative and effective methods to market your home
2. Determining asking price
3. Getting a property ready for sale
4. How to best finance your home
5. How to best negotiate with buyers and sellers
6. How to stage your home
7. Methods to cut fix-up costs
8. Methods to find buyers
9. Moving options
10. Problem solving
11. What home to buy
12. What improvements to make on a property
13. What schools have the best ratings
14. What type of home to buy
15. Where to buy

Appendix 9

Methods Your Agent Uses to Find Buyers:

1. Buyers who call on a for sale sign on a property
2. Company relocation
3. Craigs list
4. Door knocking around the property asking the neighbors who they know
5. Facebook and social media
6. Friends and family
7. From their current and past clients
8. From the parents, teachers, and faculty of the local schools
9. Newspaper ads
10. Open Houses
11. Radio, television, and YouTube
12. Real estate agents
13. Social media
14. The local businesses, such as the closest supermarket

Appendix 10

Skills Your Agent Uses to Close Your Transactions:

1. Ability to see a situation from different perspectives
2. Ability to think creatively outside the box for solutions
3. A calm demeanor in the face of hostility and disagreement
4. A love of what they are doing
5. A willingness to focus on solutions rather than being right
6. Communication with others to assist you
7. Patience to talk with and understand all sides
8. To be unstoppable
9. The generosity to give more than may be considered fair
10. The skills to get things done

Appendix 11

Here are some of the skills of professionals your agent utilizes to close your escrows:

1. Arbitrator
2. Coach
3. Connector of individuals
4. Contractor
5. Communicator
6. Counselor
7. Creative genius
8. Financier
9. Handyman
10. Jack of all trades
11. Lawyer
12. Magician
13. Negotiator
14. Politician
15. Problem solver
16. Project Manager
17. Psychologist

Appendix 12

Tasks Your Agent Manages in Handling Listings:

1. Broker open houses
2. Checking permits with the city
3. Communications with buyers, agents, and affiliates
4. Determining an estimate of value
5. Locating the property to list/market
6. Major and minor repairs
7. Meeting agents, inspectors, contractors, repair, and maintenance people
8. Negotiating contracts
9. Open houses for the public
10. Pitching the listing at association and office meetings
11. Presenting the property for sale (MLS, social media, websites, email marketing, print and electronic advertising)
12. Problem solving
13. Promoting the listing to agents
14. Settling on an asking price
15. Showings
16. Staging of the property
17. Writing the description of the property

Appendix 13

Example of a Structure for Completion for Closing an Escrow:

Closing Date	June 15th
Recording date	June 14th
Fund loan	June 13th
Submit loan for final approval	June 11th
Satisfy all loan conditions	June 10th
Receive final conditions list	June 7th
Satisfy initial conditions	June 5th
Receive initial conditions list	June 1st
Finalize loan package	May 28th
Finish processing checklist	May 25th
Complete all property inspections	May 12th
Oder all the inspections	May 8th
Begin processing loan	May 7th
Get all paperwork signed	May 6th
Open escrow	May 4th
Have all parties sign counter offers	May 3rd
Sign initial offer	May 1st

Appendix 14

Ways Your Agent Connects and Influences Others:

- To be able to create agreements
- To be bold and brave enough to risk making mistakes
- To be committed to making a difference and contribute
- To be one who puts other's needs ahead of their own
- To be open to another person's point of view
- To be real and not try to just look good, or be there for their own purposes
- To be strong enough to allow others to fully express themselves
- To be the one who makes things happen…and close most any escrow
- To engage in conversation from a space of discovery
- To every day be dynamic and excited
- To listen and speak from a space of positivity
- To really listen
- To see people as the potential for greatness they are

Appendix 15

184 TASKS An AGENT DOES FOR YOU

From the Ohio Association of Realtors Website
Written by Pat Vredevoogd-Combs, past president of the National Association of REALTORS

Pre-Listing Activities
1. Make appointment with seller for listing presentation.
2. Send a written or email confirmation of appointment and call to confirm.
3. Review appointment questions.
4. Research all comparable currently listed properties.
5. Research sales activity for past 18 months from MLS and public databases.
6. Research "average days on market" for properties similar in type, price, and location.
7. Download and review property tax roll information.
8. Prepare "comparable market analysis" (CMA) to establish market value.
9. Obtain copy of subdivision plat/complex layout.
10. Research property's ownership and deed type.
11. Research property's public record information for lot size and dimensions.
12. Verify legal description.
13. Research property's land use coding and deed restrictions.
14. Research property's current use and zoning.
15. Verify legal names of owner(s) in county's public property records.
16. Prepare listing presentation package with above materials.
17. Perform exterior "curb appeal assessment" of subject property.
18. Compile and assemble formal file on property.
19. Confirm current public schools and explain their impact on market value.
20. Review listing appointment checklist to ensure completion of all tasks.

Listing Appointment Presentation
21. Give seller an overview of current market conditions and projections.
22. Review agent and company credentials and accomplishments.
23. Present company's profile and position or "niche" in the marketplace.
24. Present CMA results, including comparables, solds, current listings and expireds.
25. Offer professional pricing strategy based and interpretation of current market conditions.

26. Discuss goals to market effectively.
27. Explain market power and benefits of multiple listing service.
28. Explain market power of web marketing, IDX, and REALTOR.com.
29. Explain the work the broker and agent do "behind the scenes" and agent's availability on weekends.
30. Explain agent's role in screening qualified buyers to protect against curiosity seekers.
31. Present and discuss strategic master marketing plan.
32. Explain different agency relationships and determine seller's preference.
33. Review all clauses in listing contract and obtain seller's signature.

After Listing Agreement is Signed
34. Review current title information.
35. Measure overall and heated square footage.
36. Measure interior room sizes.
37. Confirm lot size via owner's copy of certified survey, if available.
38. Note any and all unrecorded property lines, agreements, easements.
39. Obtain house plans, if applicable and available.
40. Review house plans, make copy.
41. Order plat map for retention in property's listing file.
42. Prepare showing instructions for buyers' agents and agree on showing time with seller.
43. Obtain current mortgage loan(s) information: companies and account numbers.
44. Verify current loan information with lender(s).
45. Check assumability of loan(s) and any special requirements.
46. Discuss possible buyer financing alternatives and options with seller.
47. Review current appraisal if available.
48. Identify Home Owner Association manager is applicable.
49. Verify Home Owner Association fees with manager–mandatory or optional and current annual fee.
50. Order copy of Home Owner Association bylaws, if applicable.
51. Research electricity availability and supplier's name and phone number.
52. Calculate average utility usage from last 12 months of bills.
53. Research and verify city sewer/septic tank system.
54. Calculate average water system fees or rates from last 12 months of bills.
55. Or confirm well status, depth, and output from Well Report.
56. Research/verify natural gas availability, supplier's name, and phone number.
57. Verify security system, term of service, and whether owned or leased.
58. Verify if seller has transferable Termite Bond.
59. Ascertain need for lead-based paint disclosure.
60. Prepare detailed list of property amenities and assess market impact.
61. Prepare detailed list of property's "Inclusions & Conveyances with Sale."

62. Complete list of completed repairs and maintenance items.
63. Send "Vacancy Checklist" to seller if property is vacant.
64. Explain benefits of Home Owner Warranty to seller.
65. Assist sellers with completion and submission of Home Owner Warranty application.
66. When received, place Home Owner Warranty in property file for conveyance at time of sale.
67. Have extra key made for lockbox.
68. Verify if property has rental units involved. And if so:
69. Make copies of all leases for retention in listing file.
70. Verify all rents and deposits.
71. Inform tenants of listing and discuss how showings will be handled.
72. Arrange for yard sign installation.
73. Assist seller with completion of Seller's Disclosure form.
74. Complete "new listing checklist."
75. Review results of Curb Appeal Assessment with seller and suggest improvements for salability.
76. Review results of Interior Decor Assessment and suggest changes to shorten time on market.
77. Load listing time into transaction management software.

Entering Property in MLS Database
78. Prepare MLS Profile Sheet–agent is responsible for "quality control" and accuracy of listing data.
79. Enter property data from Profile Sheet into MLS listing database.
80. Proofread MLS database listing for accuracy, including property placement in mapping function.
81. Add property to company's Active Listings.
82. Provide seller with signed copies of Listing Agreement and MLS Profile Data Form within 48 hours.
83. Take more photos for upload into MLS and use in flyers. Discuss efficacy of panoramic photography.

Marketing the Listing

84. Create print and Internet ads with seller's input.
85. Coordinate showings with owners, tenants, and other agents. Return all calls–weekends included.
86. Install electronic lockbox. Program with agreed-upon showing time windows.
87. Prepare mailing and contact list.
88. Generate mail-merge letters to contact list.
89. Order "Just Listed" labels and reports.
90. Prepare flyers and feedback forms.
91. Review comparable MLS listings regularly to ensure property remains competitive in price, terms, conditions, and availability.
92. Prepare property marketing brochure for seller's review.
93. Arrange for printing or copying of supply of marketing brochures or flyers.

94. Place marketing brochures in all company agent mailboxes.

95. Upload listing to company and agent Internet sites, if applicable.

96. Mail "Just Listed" notice to all neighborhood residents.

97. Advise Network Referral Program of listing.

98. Provide marketing data to buyers from international relocation networks.

99. Provide marketing data to buyers coming from referral network.

100. Provide "Special Feature" cards form marketing, if applicable/

101. Submit ads to company's participating Internet real estate sites.

102. Convey price changes promptly to all Internet groups.

103. Reprint/supply brochures promptly as needed.

104. Review and update loan information in MLS as required.

105. Send feedback emails/faxes to buyers' agents after showings.

106. Review weekly Market Study.

107. Discuss feedback from showing agents with seller to determine if changes will accelerate the sale.

108. Place regular weekly update calls to seller to discuss marketing and pricing.

109. Promptly enter price changes in MLS listings database.

The Offer and the Contract

110. Receive and review all Offer to Purchase contracts submitted by buyers or buyers' agents.

111. Evaluate offer(s) and prepare "net sheet" on each for owner to compare.

112. Counsel seller on offers. Explain merits and weakness of each component of each offer.

113. Contact buyers' agents to review buyer's qualifications and discuss offer.

114. Fax/deliver Seller's Disclosure to buyer's agent or buyer upon request and prior to offer if possible.

115. Confirm buyer is pre-qualified by calling loan officer.

116. Obtain pre-qualification letter on buyer from loan officer.

117. Negotiate all offers on seller's behalf, setting time limit for loan approval and closing date.

118. Prepare and convey any counteroffers, acceptance, or amendments to buyer's agent.

119. Fax copies of contract and all addendums to closing attorney or title company.

120. When Offer-to-Purchase contract is accepted and signed by seller, deliver to buyer's agent.

121. Record and promptly deposit buyer's money into escrow account.

122. Disseminate "Under-Contract Showing Restrictions" as seller requests.

123. Deliver copies of fully signed Offer to Purchase contract to sellers.

124. Fax/deliver copies of Offer to Purchase contract to selling agent.

125. Fax copies of Offer to Purchase contract to lender.

126. Provide copies of signed Offer to Purchase contract for office file.

127. Advise seller in handling additional offers to purchase submitted between contract and closing.

128. Change MLS status to "Sale Pending."

129. Update transaction management program to show "Sale Pending."

130. Review buyer's credit report results–Advise seller of worst and best case scenarios.

131. Provide credit report information to seller if property is to be seller-financed.

132. Assist buyer with obtaining financing and follow up as necessary.

133. Coordinate with lender on discount points being locked in with dates.

134. Deliver unrecorded property information to buyer.

135. Order septic inspection, if applicable.

136. Receive and review septic system report and access any impact on sale.

137. Deliver copy of septic system inspection report to lender and buyer.

138. Deliver well flow test report copies to lender, buyer, and listing file.

139. Verify termite inspection ordered.

140. Verify mold inspection ordered, if required.

Tracking the Loan Process

141. Confirm return of verifications of deposit and buyer's employment.

142. Follow loan processing through to the underwriter.

143. Add lender and other vendors to transaction management program so agents, buyer, and seller can track progress of sale.

144. Contact lender weekly to ensure processing is on track.

145. Relay final approval of buyer's loan application to seller.

Home Inspection

146. Coordinate buyer's professional home inspection with seller.

147. Review home inspector's report.

148. Enter completion into transaction management tracking software program.

149. Explain seller's responsibilities of loan limits and interpret any clauses in the contract.

150. Ensure seller's compliance with home inspection clause requirements.

151. Assist seller with identifying and negotiating with trustworthy contractors for required repairs.

152. Negotiate payment and oversee completion of all required repairs on seller's behalf, if needed.

The Appraisal

153. Schedule appraisal.

154. Provide comparable sales used in market pricing to appraiser.

155. Follow up on appraisal.

156. Enter completion into transaction management program.

157. Assist seller in questioning appraisal report if it seems too low.

Closing Preparations and Duties

158. Make sure contract is signed by all parties.
159. Coordinate closing process with buyer's agent and lender.
160. Update closing forms and files.
161. Ensure all parties have all forms and information needed to close the sale.
162. Select location for closing.
163. Confirm closing date and time and notify all parties.
164. Solve any title problems (boundary disputes, easements, etc.) or in obtaining death certificates.
165. Work with buyer's agent in scheduling and conducting buyer's final walkthrough prior to closing.
166. Research all tax, HOA, utility, and other applicable prorations.
167. Request final closing figures from closing agent (attorney or title company).
168. Receive and carefully review closing figures to ensure accuracy.
169. Forward verified closing figures to buyer's agent.
170. Request copy of closing documents from closing agent.
171. Confirm the buyer and buyer's agent received title insurance commitment.
172. Provide "Home Owners Warranty" for availability at closing.
173. Review all closing documents carefully for errors.
174. Forward closing documents to absentee seller as requested.
175. Review documents with closing agent (attorney).
176. Provide earnest money deposit from escrow account to closing agent.
177. Coordinate closing with seller's next purchase, resolving timing issues.
178. Have a "no surprises" closing so that seller receives a net proceeds check at closing.
179. Refer sellers to one of the best agents at their destination, if applicable.
180. Change MLS status to Sold. Enter sale date, price, selling broker and agent's ID numbers, etc.
181. Close out listing in transaction management program.

Follow Up After Closing

182. Answer questions about filing claims with Home Owner Warranty company, if requested.
183. Attempt to clarify and resolve any repair conflicts if buyer is dissatisfied.
184. Respond to any follow-up calls and provide any additional information required from office files.

Appendix 16

Your agent will assist you by:

1. allowing you to express your concerns.

2. assisting you in choosing the best available options.

3. assisting you in seeing your choices.

4. being there so you can simply talk about what matters to you.

5. coming up with solutions to problems.

6. giving you space to state your frustrations.

7. helping you see the bigger picture.

Appendix 17

Pre-interview checklist:

1. Call at least two of their testimonials to verify their authenticity.

2. Has the prospective agent passed the text test?

3. Have they passed your Google search?

4. Locate a potential agent.

5. Review their testimonials.

6. View their website. Did they pass your criteria?

Glossary

Affiliate: the professionals who work with your real estate agent, they include escrow officers, title, termite, lender, and home protection representatives.

Agent: a person who is authorized to act for or represent another.

Appraisal: an opinion of value based upon a factual analysis.

Broker: one who is licensed by the state to carry on the business of dealing in real estate.

Broker open house: an open house mostly for agents to view the home, food is often served as an incentive for agents to come.

Closer: slang for someone who completes, or puts a sale together.

Closing: the completion of a sale or escrow to the point of recording the deed with the county recorder's office.

Considerations: anything which is, legally, of value and induces one to enter into a contract.

Deal: slang for a transaction, or where an agreement has been settled upon.

Default: stop paying back a loan as to the agreed terms.

Escrow: the period of time between when a property goes pending and it actually closes escrow and title is transferred.

Expired: a property whose listing period has been completed and not renewed by the same brokerage.

Fiduciary: one acting in a relationship of trust regarding financial transactions.

Fixture: personal property that is attached to real property and is legally considered real property while it is so attached.

FSBO: For Sale By Owner.

Funding: where a lender approves a loan and places the money (funds) in an escrow.

Interest Rates: the percentage of an amount of money that is paid for its use for a specified time.

Inventory: real estate term for all the homes for sale in a given area.

Listing: a property that is on the market for sale is called a listing.

Lenders: the individuals and their companies who handle the obtaining of the loan for the purchase and refinance of real estate.

Loan Documents: the paperwork signed regarding the loan prior to funding and closing.

Loan Conditions: items that are required by the lender/underwriter to satisfy themselves to the credit worthiness of a buyer.

Market: the whole of the properties for sale at a given time in a given area.

MLS: Multiple Listing Service, an entry that serves to make the property information available to view.

NAR: National Association of Realtors

Neighborhood Specialist: a real estate agent who does most of their work in a particular small geographic area or neighborhood and is most familiar with the prices, types, and models of properties, the schools, business, and people.

Open House: making a home available for viewing for the public, signs are placed around the property to guide people to the location.

Pending: a property that has been sold and hasn't yet closed escrow.

Property: anything that is owned by someone, also see Real Estate.

Real Estate: land and anything permanently affixed to land, such as a home or building.

Sold: a property that has been purchased by a buyer and has closed escrow.

Stage: getting a property ready for sale by eliminating clutter, cleaning and arranging the furniture, painting, etc., to make the home as presentable as possible.

Terms: the considerations, other than price for sale or lease. For example, the way the money will be paid, time to take possession, considerations, etc.

Transaction: the process of taking a sale from an agreement to closing.

Underwriter: one who ensures another, an underwriter is the person or person's who determine if a loan will be approved or not approved.

About the Author

David Kline Lovett began his real estate career in 1977 when he bought his first property at the age of twenty-one. David earned his real estate license in 1979 and became a successful full-time agent in 1984. In 2004 David became a real estate broker in order to further his knowledge to better serve his clients. In 2016 David found, studied, and learned the 7 secret strategies for a buyer and 9 secret strategies for a seller to save tens of thousands when you buy or sell.

David is also a writer, musician, coach, healer, comedian and speaker. David is primarily invested, interested, and excited to be assisting others to realize their goals, dreams, & full self expression. You can view additional transformational tools at the beginning of this book, or go to:
dklhomes.com and
davidklinelovett.com
godimhappy@me.com